T0222639

PATTERNS OF SOFTWARE CONSTRUCTION

HOW TO PREDICTABLY BUILD RESULTS

Stephen Rylander

Apress®

Patterns of Software Construction: How to Predictably Build Results

Stephen Rylander
Glen Ellyn, IL, USA

ISBN-13 (pbk): 978-1-4842-7935-9   ISBN-13 (electronic): 978-1-4842-7936-6
https://doi.org/10.1007/978-1-4842-7936-6

Managing Director, Apress Media LLC: Welmoed Spahr
Acquisitions Editor: Shiva Ramachandran
Development Editor: James Markham
Coordinating Editor: Jessica Vakili

Distributed to the book trade worldwide by Springer Science+Business Media New York, 1 New York Plaza, New York, NY 100043. Phone 1-800-SPRINGER, fax (201) 348-4505, e-mail orders-ny@springer-sbm.com, or visit www.springeronline.com. Apress Media, LLC is a California LLC and the sole member (owner) is Springer Science + Business Media Finance Inc (SSBM Finance Inc). SSBM Finance Inc is a Delaware corporation.

For information on translations, please e-mail booktranslations@springernature.com; for reprint, paperback, or audio rights, please e-mail bookpermissions@springernature.com.

Apress titles may be purchased in bulk for academic, corporate, or promotional use. eBook versions and licenses are also available for most titles. For more information, reference our Print and eBook Bulk Sales web page at http://www.apress.com/bulk-sales.

Any source code or other supplementary material referenced by the author in this book is available to readers on GitHub via the book's product page, located at https://github.com/ Apress/ Patterns-of-Software-Construction. For more detailed information, please visit http://www.apress.com/source-code.

Printed on acid-free paper

Contents

About the Author

Stephen Rylander is currently SVP, Global Head of Engineering at Donnelley Financial Solutions (DFIN). He is a software engineer–turned technical executive who has seen a variety of industries from music to ecommerce to finance and more. He is invested in improving the practice of software delivery, operational platforms, and all the people involved in making this happen. He has worked on platforms handling millions of daily transactions and developed digital transformation programs driving financial platforms. He has also had the opportunity to construct platforms with digital investing advice engines and has a history of dealing with scale and delivering results leading local and distributed teams.

Acknowledgments

I am thankful to my wonderful, smart, and beautiful wife for giving me support in writing this book. Her support in this endeavor was critical. I also give thanks here to those who believed in me, coached me, and generally "gave me a shot." Thank you Vivek Vaid, Greg Goff, Mitch Shue, James McClamroch, Perry Marchant, and Floyd Strimling. Also, a big thank you to my dad, who was always full of love and encouragement. And last, but in no way least, I am forever grateful for the coaching and education from Garret J. White, the founder of Warrior training. His coaching and systems showed me I could write this book. Thank you.

Introduction

This book started out of patterns and practices that I use in my software engineering and leadership practice. The patterns were found in the wild and honed through trial, error, success, and repetition.

I wrote this book to help you, the reader, avoid the same common pitfalls that myself and peers continuously experience. If you are an experienced practitioner of software engineering and delivery, this book will help you follow a system that works using modern practices and pragmatic decision-making. If you are new to the industry, this book allows you to see the problems that are coming for you down the road.

Yes, the same problems are coming! Generation and youth can't save you – because software is written by people and paid for with budgets – sorry. But read this book and steel yourself. Now is your opportunity to take hard lessons learned and apply them in a systematic way that will provide wisdom beyond your years.

All in all, this book is not just a collection of patterns. There is a pattern to the patterns – and I call this entire system **LIFT Engineering**. We get into the details of LIFT immediately in Chapter 1.

Thank you for reading. I hope this system and the guidance inside serves you well!

Patterns

This book describes a comprehensive process for software engineering called LIFT. LIFT is not a process. LIFT is not a methodology. LIFT is not something you read and put on a shelf. It's also not made up as you go. This is a system designed to tie a series of activities together that don't often get the attention they need during the construction of software-intensive systems. This book is not a series of individually written chapters edited together. Instead, it's cohesive in nature to help you succeed at the business of constructing and operating software. This is your software construction system.

Not a Process

It's not a process for planning a product portfolio. It's not a process for identifying market gaps or identifying breakout ideas. It's not a process to accelerate user design or validate product ideas. It's none of these.

It's also not an open process that you then plug your processes into. It's not SAFe or scaled agile, it's not scrum or lean or kanban. It's not an agile process or framework at all.

It's not a process for building products. Or great products. Or products that wow and amaze.

© Stephen Rylander 2022
S. Rylander, *Patterns of Software Construction*,
https://doi.org/10.1007/978-1-4842-7936-6_1

System

It's a system for building software that works. Constructing software. Testing it. Managing change. Releasing software. And then operating the software. That's it. LIFT is concerned with how the activities are accomplished so that they are repeatable.

The Problem

A tremendous amount of literature exists on agile product development as well as lean product development and a hundred other terms all geared on principles. Almost all these agile development frameworks/systems/ philosophies require teams to adopt and customize. Adopting something off the shelf or more likely a blog/website is tough. Once you need to customize it, it starts to fall apart at the seams.

Craftsmanship Doesn't Help

Parts of the software industry perpetuate this idea of craftsmanship, which by now has lost much of its momentum. They say software should be well honed like a craftsman would their leatherwork, tanning and stretching a hide to make units ready to be dyed, cut, and formed into various useful things. The craftsman works their woodworking bench – they know where every tool is, what they do, and when to use it. Craftsmanship is noble. Craftsmanship is modern. Craftsmanship is ascribing credence to things we want in our lives through our work, even if often at odds with the goal.

In software, this comes to bare through practices like pair programming and test-driven development – and probably a handful more. But, top-level, these are the core practices. The idea is that writing prescriptive and descriptive tests over your code is what a craftsman (person) would do. Each function has a purpose – each line of code matters. Nothing is just whipped out or copy/pasted into place. Each method makes sense in the broader context, and software patterns are applied.

The notion that software is craft has always been tenuous.

Look at the movement's history – a break from the agile practice folks, who only cared for process and not software, meant physically writing software required a name. Something special to call its own. But writing software is writing software. It doesn't matter if thousands of scrum masters have conferences – that doesn't ship software. Engineers ship software by putting hands on keyboards, testing, discussing, and project managing software.

Consider this, when was the last time two scrum masters got together and created a startup that made millions of dollars? How about two software developers? These are entirely different stories.

Therefore, there is less craft than it appears. Considering how subjectively complicated software is, it cannot easily be craft. Case in point, software that scales is the sign of success commercially. But small-batch cheese craft is coveted because it doesn't scale. Thus, the dichotomy.

Reality

Times are lean. Only the biggest, best, and wealthiest organizations can afford massive engineering teams of the best engineers globally. Their large mass creates a strong gravitational field pulling in engineers from all over the globe as you can see in Figure 1-1.

Figure 1-1. Gravity pulls talent towards the center

Not only that, but these massive organizations also deploy agile coaches and project teams to run deliveries. Or they have such a modern, scalable architecture, hundreds of small teams can act somewhat autonomously, and they don't need to scale together. And finally, massive, well financed teams have the advantage with the capacity to custom build internal software, monitoring and deployment systems. Consider the number of open-source projects just out of Netflix during the past 10 years. These are material advantages.

Managers and leaders outside of these spheres need an advantage. You know you're one of these managers when a third or more of your team is offshore, you have constrained budgets not based on your team's success or the primary purpose of the organization is not the software you build. These managers and leaders need a toolkit and a process (the system) which ties the activities of software engineering together into something that is prescriptive, efficient, repeatable, and operable. Figure 1-2 illustrates these four primary challenges.

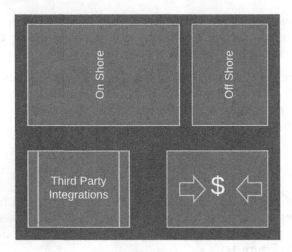

Figure 1-2. We need software to last 5–10 years to get a real return on investment

The Solution

LIFT is focused on **objective** measurements, **repeatable** activities, and the **full** life cycle of software engineering. Philosophies and case studies are fine. But actions count more. And outcomes are the only thing that matters in the game of software. It either works or it doesn't work.

> *In preparing for battle I have always found that plans are useless, but planning is indispensable.*

> —Dwight D. Eisenhower

Are your problems upfront in how work is understood before it's developed? Look at the LIFT Planning phase for an approach.

Are your problems in the construction of software and that it's always a scramble? Too slow? Unpredictable? Then look to the LIFT Build phase which provides the template for repeatable execution.

Product development challenges are not uniform. However, the scope of the challenges is known. Even though LIFT is a total system, you may choose to focus heavily on one area over another – and that's fine.

LIFT is designed to give leaders and teams a "lift" so that they don't have to reinvent the "how to" for each activity in planning, building, and operating software over and over. Or worse, read blogs on what some small team in a top-3-big-tech company did and then try to replicate it – ending in predictable failure. LIFT operates in 90% of the software space – not unicorns.

Boat crew six, you better start putting out!

—SEAL Instructor, BUDS (*Extreme Ownership*)

LIFT is made up of the following evolutions:

1. Plan

2. Build

3. Test

4. Release

5. Operate

6. Manage

It's easy to think of the six evolutions using a block diagram, like Figure 1-3.

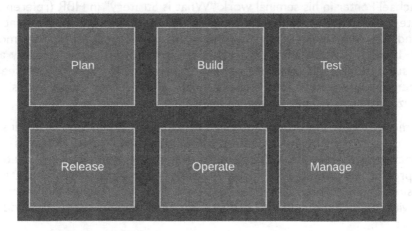

Figure 1-3. Lift Evolutions Overview

Each evolution is made up of a series of activities. *How these activities are performed, the details of each and when to do them is the primary purpose of LIFT.* Executing on any one of these evolutions on their own will give you benefit from where you are today. But it's how the activities (illustrated in Figure 1-4) are tied together into one system that will raise your team and provide material, long term, repeatable results.

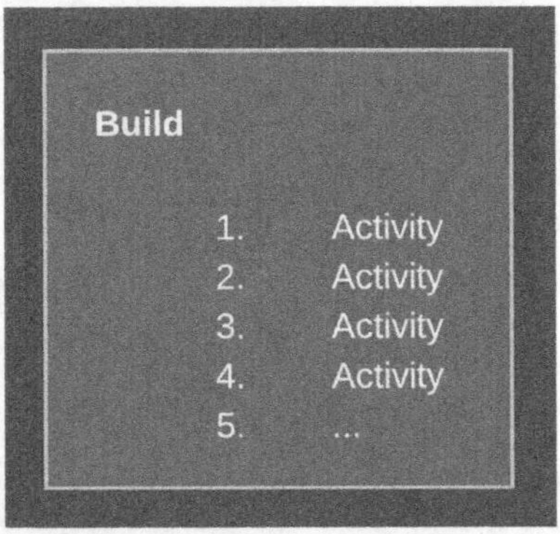

Figure 1-4. These activities are what LIFT is focused on because it is what is most variable between team to team and project to project

Further, building software systems requires a formulated strategy. According to Michael Porter in his seminal work "What is Strategy" in HBR (reference), "Strategy is creating fit among a company's activities. The success of a strategy depends on doing many things well - not just a few - and integrating among them. If there is no fit among activities, there is no distinctive strategy and little sustainability. Management reverts to the simpler task of overseeing independent functions and operational effectiveness determines an organization's relative performance."

LIFT models some of Porter's approach by forcing the activities to live inside evolutions – and then tying these evolutions together. Figure 1-5 shows how connecting the evolutions in turn connects the end-to-end delivery strategy. The project is figuratively climbing the mountain, to a new peak, repeatedly. And since the numerous activities are tucked nicely into evolutions, there are less wires to connect and the process becomes easier to envision and to execute.

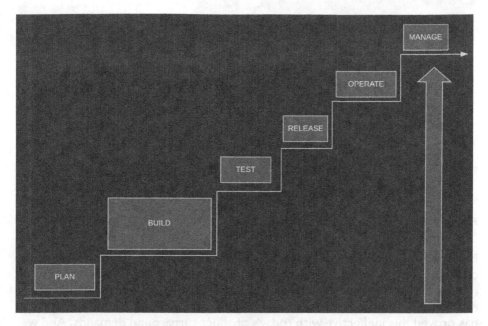

Figure 1-5. Climbing the evolutionary mountain

Porter's examination of an entire corporation can be applied to a product engineering department, mid-size organization, or anyone building internal IT systems. Excellence at only the release portion of the life cycle, or the test portion will not deliver big results. It probably won't even deliver the required business results. And if each link in the chain doesn't connect with the next, then the entire chain is brittle. Not having these activities clearly operationalized, systematized, and repeatable also means that the team will silo themselves. This then has managers attempting to optimize only their areas (development, operations, test), or exec teams trying to optimize for them and trying to then drive cost efficiencies. This will not lead to a competitive advantage. It just leads to leaner vertical, independent functions.

Rinse and Repeat

Like any good system, LIFT is repeatable. Figure 1-6 shows the repetition of evolutions.

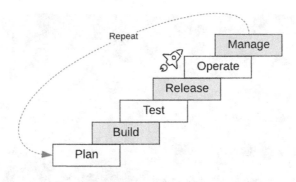

6 Evolutions = 1 System Cycle

Figure 1-6. The evolutions create a system cycle

Now that we understand Porter's intent behind a formulated strategy, it's clear why an evolutionary strategy with software system development is required. We cannot waterfall software development by loading all requirements at once and then delivering a big bang at the end – the industry has proved this ineffective with today's product turnaround demands. And we can't rely on agile consulting to continuously build "what the customer wants" because this process is more expensive up front than it sounds and often causes massive friction against internal organizational structures. Instead, like in Figure 1-6, we incrementally build the parts of our software system and release. The cadence of the system is to build and release.

■ **Note**   Ten out of ten readers of this chapter will have an opinion on waterfall, so let's clear the deck for the rest of this book. Waterfall is not sequentially writing code, testing, and releasing. What can be wrong with that? How does one test code that is not written or release code that is not tested? No. Waterfall is the complete upfront end to end plan with very little flex in the joints and expecting the entire system to integrate and test successfully at the end. It is not evolutionary. It is more like the big bang of the universe – there was nothing and then there was software in production. And it doesn't work.

LIFT gives attention to all the pieces that make up the trivialization of software construction. Testing is difficult. Releasing is often complex. Operating a production system is hazardous. And managing the overall process and people to do this work is complex at the least and chaotic at the worst.

Thinking about software construction as six evolutions that make up one system cycle, which is then repeatable, gives this required formulated strategy a backbone to the entire endeavor of software construction.

Getting Started

Things You May Need

Prerequisites for Lowest Friction

1. Your teams (entire engineering organization) are broken up into squads, if you are operating with 10 or more full time engineers (developers, testing, UX, etc.).

2. There is someone playing product owner representing product management.

3. Someone plays the role of a scrum master, for example, daily coordination facilitator.

Or Not

If you don't have the prerequisites, you can still be very successful with this system. Almost all other literature on running flexible, modern engineering projects specifies these roles be filled by someone full time. This is just not reality. Teams all over are strapped for time and resources and having a product owner separate from a product manager is rarer than it sounds when reading online articles.

© Stephen Rylander 2022
S. Rylander, *Patterns of Software Construction*,
https://doi.org/10.1007/978-1-4842-7936-6_2

This system is not tied to agile, waterfall, water-scrum-fall, or scrumerfall. LIFT is how we build software; therefore, it is compatible with where you are right now and your team structures. More than anything, LIFT will help you get started, past the paralysis and into healthy motion.

Must Haves

- A work management tool (Jira, Azure Boards, etc.).

- A backlog of work functioning as some sort of requirements. This can be in the form of a digital backlog in your work management tool or written set of user stories, or a set of feature requirements written up and organized into a document.

- A clear Product Roadmap that the team understands.

Charter

Before we get to the evolutions of LIFT, there is an additional concept that is very effective no matter the size of the project: a project charter document.

Don't let the idea of "yet another" document worry you – this one is written with the intent to reduce scope. Yes, this is the primary scope reduction document – and that is something to be excited about... so don't let the opportunity pass.

The Charter lays out the goals of the project, the desired outcomes, what isn't required, known dependencies, and risks. It provides a guiding direction for the team working on the project as the common understanding is derived from this simple document. There isn't more direction on this because it's meant to be simple. Table 2-1 shows a basic outline you can use or download a copy from the LIFT Engineering site.

Table 2-1. A basic project charter

Business case	In-scope/out-of-scope
•	-
Problem statement	-
•	...
Solution	Risks
•	-
Timeline	-
•	Project team and stakeholders
Goals and success criteria	• Lead
-	• Team members
-	• ...
...	
Assumptions, constraints, and dependencies	
•	

Architecture

The topic of topics. Architecture. What is architecture, what isn't architecture? Who makes these decisions and how are they introduced into a system? LIFT is not concerned.

LIFT is concerned about two concepts of architecture, if and only if there is a required change to the architecture. This is

1. The Current State of the Architecture

2. The Future State of the Architecture

That's it. What happens with architectural choices, for many services, one service, no APIs, tons of APIs, monolith, or distributed system matters very little. It's all execution details at one point or another. Wait, take a breath. It's OK – it really is just details when looked at from a high enough level.

The question is if the concepts can be captured into a view that will help the project team design, build, test, deliver, and operate the system be it net-new or updates to the existing system.

Let's play this through just a bit. Let's say, the new project, Project Boots, is a product with (1) one web front end and (2) one small API layer and (3) one database. The team analyzes the new requirements and sees that they will need to add a couple new APIs that are asynchronous connecting to third-party services. Because of this new behavior they will introduce these APIs into a different container from the existing APIs. The architecture has evolved, the core concepts are the same, but there are now new pieces. Figure 2-1 shows a current state architecture and Figure 2-2 shows the evolved future state architecture.

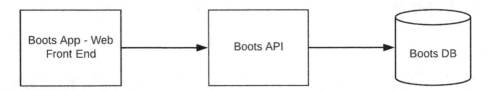

Figure 2-1. This is a super-simplified Current State Architecture view. Web front end, API, and a database

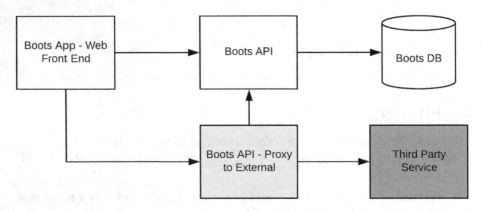

Figure 2-2. This is the Future State Architecture view

Here, in Figure 2-2, it's clear what the changes are because they are highlighted. Almost anyone from a junior developer to a group head can read something like this and grasp the change. From here, the discussion of infrastructure, security, and operations can start. This will win you many friends in your current team and your career. And, most importantly, it will set the project up for success by removing early project friction and confusion.

Like the Charter, another series of chapters could be written on *Current vs. Future State Architectures*, so we won't go there. This concept is simple. Just let it stay simple and don't overcomplicate it.

Mindset to Bring

Each evolution in LIFT is about small, consistent steps. An evolution is made up of activities. Each activity has steps to take. It's not about running the marathon – it's about running the next mile and the next mile and the next mile. By the end, you ran the marathon. And you got there because you knew where the finish line was. You didn't just run in circles hoping to go 26.2 miles.

Focus on the next step to get to the next evolution.

Every time you execute the system, through the six evolutions, you will put work items in the next release/iteration which improve the overall process and your software for the next round. Therefore, this mindset is *continuous improvement.*

Keep improving what you have.

The next mindset is *organization*. This will serve the execution of the evolutions. Next is *discipline*. Discipline will allow you to execute the activities in each evolution even when you think it can be skipped. And attention to *detail* will serve the overall success of the project because details are the difference between success and failure, being an amateur and being a professional.

Details Matter.

Summary: Focus on the next step, continuous improvement, organization, discipline, and details matter.

The difference between a boiling pot of water and warm water is only one degree.

Definitions

Term	Definition
Tech Lead	A tech lead is someone in the development team who can operate with the product owner and other stakeholders. This role is usually writing software, but sometimes it's a manager who is a little less hands on.
Product Owner	This individual directs what the work is and the general sequencing of customer facing delivery. They must find the requirements, document them in the work management tool.
Document	A document is any digital, or physical, set of notes and descriptions for a particular set of work.
Backlog	The backlog, as used in this context, refers to a backlog of user stories/epics/features in a work management tool (WMT) or just a set of requirements in some other format.

(continued)

Term	Definition
Work Item	Any digital representation of a task, user story, tech story, backlog item.
Steel Thread	A development approach building small pieces of all non-functional requirements to exercise the entire system.
Big Rock	Complex, high effort, high reward work.

System Evolutions

Plan

Evolution #1

The Plan evolution in LIFT starts after the "we know what we want to build" phase of your overall product planning process. The planning here consists of taking a backlog of requirements, product desires with an architecture overview and translating that into a releasable version of a software product.

The releases may be immediately consumed by users, in a silent deployed state or released into an upstream integration environment with other teams. The point is: this is planning to start construction of one or more incremental software releases – not planning for a year or executing a portfolio of projects. The scope and focus are important for success. Success is in the details.

© Stephen Rylander 2022
S. Rylander, *Patterns of Software Construction*,
https://doi.org/10.1007/978-1-4842-7936-6_3

Category	Description
Target	A clear, actionable, set of releases the team can start slicing apart
Inputs	Your backlog or set of requirements for a release
Outputs	1. A sliced-up release plan, with more than one delivery phase containing pieces of all non-functional requirements
	2. One document outlining the release plan
	3. Work items loaded into your work management tool
	4. Sequenced plan for Building
Visibility	Work items loaded into your work management tool (WMT)
The Win	Confidence that the steel thread execution plan will end with working software, including non-functional requirements, exercising the different parts of the system and the business features

You're at the start of your project. At this point, you have a backlog of work – something that needs to get done. The first step is to look at this backlog and figure out what's releasable, in what order, and what it will take to accomplish that.

Target

Step one is to identify your target. What is your goal? Write it down and make it clear so everyone agrees.

For instance, "the target of this release is enabling our professional services team to configure the user management screens for a customer." This is challenging, has a purpose, and is not overly prescriptive.

Anti-Pattern! Heads Up!

Beware the overly prescriptive business feature that is just telling the engineering team not only what to implement, but how. An anti-pattern is a release goal like "enable the new technical widget across all pages of the application."

That's tough. And just begging to fail. A widget is almost always some technical component. And "all" pages? Really? And for what purpose? Just rip out the old widget and replace? There isn't any new functionality? Test cases? Users? Screens? Nothing?

Success is found in the details. You may have to coach the business target into something more like "upgrade the most used pages in the app so we can authorize content in the widget like the page." Why? Because our customers need more granular security because of what we learned about how they use the software.

Map It Out

Step two is to take your user activities (or system activities, same in the context of LIFT) and map out a visualization of these. These activities may come from feature lists or a document of bulleted requirements for user activities. If you don't have this, then that's a problem and it will be a struggle to proceed. These are a part of the Inputs to the Plan Evolution we are in. Go back and get them.

You can do the mapping on a whiteboard, stickies, in software – it doesn't matter. What's important is to capture the activities moving left to right on what you're trying to accomplish. Think wide and shallow first. This forms a backbone for the work.

Then, and only then, start thinking about and filling in the details. It will look a little like Figure 3-1. There are probably cards that say things like

- Wire up our logging library to login page
- Update deploy script for dev environment
- Show a static grid on the dashboard screen

Figure 3-1. Mapping out all activities that make up releases

Now, the activities laid out in Figure 3-1 can be anything. What's important is capturing the activities so that light is cast onto not just the business functionality, but the work and activities to make these ideas come to life.

This is an ideal format for engineers to express the need for non-functional requirements, or simply capture the effort to get a minimum-ready-release state.

Finally, slice releases out of the work (Figure 3-2), where a release is working software delivered to your stage, UAT, or live environment.

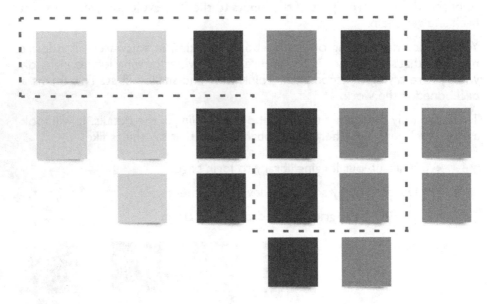

Figure 3-2. Slicing out releases from activity mapping

■ **Note** Why do we say stage, UAT, or live? Because every team has a different set of environments for different reasons. And those reasons don't matter. LIFT assists in filling the basics with patterns and proven steps. In this case, a team may have deliveries to stage and, then after accumulating two or three of those, feel like they have enough to go live. Or maybe your product is already mature, and these features are going straight out to users. Either case will work.

There is an excellent book on this topic of planning called *User Story Mapping* by Jeff Patton.

Now, if this is your very first construction phase of a new product, please consider identifying the absolute smallest product you could build which would exercise end to end functionality. Small. Like really small. This is possibly a web page that says "hello world" with React, calling a Java API that writes a message to a database that says "hello" and logs the activity. Then deploy that to dev. Why? Because it tested N pieces of the system, proves your build pipelines work and that it will work somewhere besides a laptop.

Development Strategy

Over and over, we will refer to the preferred development strategy as Steel Thread. This development strategy says that we'll take just enough of all the major functional and non-functional pieces of a story to make it usable. We will go much deeper on this in the Build Evolution. For now, know that the development strategy is to use a steel thread and *progressively mature the feature.*

Big Rocks

Big Rocks is the LIFT way of interpreting the famous concept of *First Things First.* Now, *First Things First* was not invented here. This concept was first written by Stephen R. Covey — a great thinker of the human condition and productivity.

This principle is so basic, but so important, it's good to take a few moments to review using an analogy of filling a bucket.

- Big Rocks are the highest priority tasks and projects.
- Little Rocks are urgent items. You must do them at some point, or you'll get overrun by them.
- Sand is everything unimportant that doesn't materially move you, the team, or product forward.

So, what does this have to do with developing software? Everything. The Big Rocks in your project are the most important and difficult tasks. An example of a Big Rock is "integrate the new Global Authentication System for Role Management." Or "build a proxy to the new Pricing API that returns under 5ms." This is non-trivial work! Most mid-size, 3–6-month projects, have at least 2–3 Big Rocks.

And the thing is, we must get after the Big Rocks first because they are the most challenging, will require the most effort, and have the highest risk of failure, which brings us back to "First Things First." It's a waste of time to prioritize your schedule. You have to schedule your priorities. This is why the Big Rocks must go first. See the graphic in Figure 3-3.

Pebbles First   Rocks First

Figure 3-3. Big rocks first

Like I said, it's simple. If the pebbles and sand go in first the big rocks won't fit. If the rocks go in first, then the pebbles and sand can flow around it, and everything fits. Success with LIFT means putting the Big Rocks first and going after them intentionally.

> *Effective leadership is putting first things first. Effective management is discipline; carrying it out.*
>
> —Stephen R. Covey

Write the Stories

LIFT has adopted the agile term "story" or "user story" because it's so prevalent in the industry. Substitute your own word or phrase if it makes it easier for you when communicating with your team.

Now that you have a few releases sliced out, write the stories. How you write the stories is outside of the scope for LIFT, but just make sure they are

1. Actionable.

2. Specific.

3. Completable with the development strategy.

4. Have dependencies called out.

5. Testable with test criteria.

6. Entered and organized into your WMT as epics, features, or some other grouping. It's sometimes helpful just to put them all into a Release.

Test Criteria?

The debate on where test criteria goes to is a waste of time. The **testing criteria for a story goes into the story** in the work management tool. It doesn't matter if it's called "acceptance criteria," "test steps," or "expected results." The criteria of how to test and the results of the test are captured in the story. This keeps everything about a particular story together.

What about bigger stories? There is no such thing as a big story. This is a smell that your story is doing too much.

What about capturing lengthy details and diagrams on complex processes? This is not a story level concern. Document these narratives and system designs in another tool and put the link in the story for reference.

Build the Sequence

LIFT Engineering uses all good tools at our disposal. A key, powerful tool are basic Gantt charts. A basic Gantt chart allows you to sequence work, show dependencies, communicate plans to stakeholders, and understand when things are going off the rails. You don't need to run the whole world from your Gantt chart (or call it a technical sequencing diagram if it makes you feel better...), but it will be invaluable if you are

1. Building software with multiple dependencies

2. Building software with more than one team or functional parts of an organization

3. Building software with distributed teams

4. Building software that is time constrained

So, it's almost always helpful. Figure 3-4 illustrates a basic example.

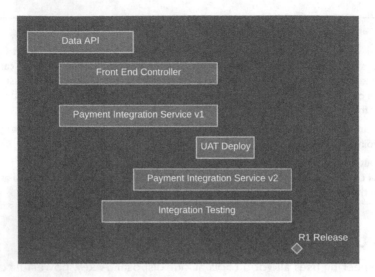

Figure 3-4. Gannt charts help visualize the sequence of activities

Summary

Here are the patterns to learn:

- Map out the project from what you know
- How to design for the Steel Thread
- Identifying Big Rocks
- Sequencing the work

It's important to deploy these technical patterns to avoid the agile Hamster Wheel effect described here.

Agile Hamster Wheel

The Agile Hamster Wheel effect is when a development team feels like they are doing the same thing over and over. There are no breaks. No seams to pull apart.

Life becomes one big backlog – groom, build, plan, release, groom, build, plan, over and over. When this happens, the technical platform can suffer. There isn't room in there to think. That's why the patterns of slicing work into releases via steel threads is important. This makes sure that the non-functional requirements don't get thrown away or that features without entry points don't get deployed.

Lastly, lots of teams are doing their retrospectives (post-release review, etc.) in the same stale way every time – so the team needs to mix up how they perform these rituals. It's just one quick Google search away. If the team feels like life is this rut, try putting in a couple break days between sprints to take a breath to think about the future.

Activities Summary

- Slice work into releases.
    - Identify product features that are most important.
    - Go left to right on them.
    - Slice out the releases.
    - Development strategy: Find the steel thread on tech that ties them together.
    - Starting with a 4-cycle engine before building a race car engine. Basic logging. Something reads from the database. Basic.
    - It's more like color by number. Do all the 1's. Then all the 2's. Then all the 3's.
    - Build a basic wall board. (optional)

- Identify your Big Rocks.

- Convert your releasable steel thread into stories for each delivery making up a release. Load them into the WMT.

- Build a basic Gantt showing sequencing and dependencies. You will most likely have dependencies if you work in an organization with more than 20 engineers.

- It's a pattern. Learn the pattern. You learn by building up reps so get to it.

Build

Evolution #2

In the build evolution, the team constructs software using the best techniques available to them. LIFT is not prescriptive of how to write code. Here, we will examine what most software looks like and extract patterns to consistently win this evolution. And even though agile is not a panacea, some of the techniques are helpful and the terms are common enough not to redefine them – starting with what a sprint looks like in the LIFT world.

Category	Description
Target	Increments of working software as close to the live environment as possible.
Inputs	Sliced up release plan stitched together with a steel thread approach.
	High-level work-items in your WMT.
Outputs	A releasable version of software.
Visibility	Clear view of WIP, velocity, and defects in WMT.
The Win	You have Working Software in a non-dev environment that has been tested successfully.

© Stephen Rylander 2022

S. Rylander, *Patterns of Software Construction*,

https://doi.org/10.1007/978-1-4842-7936-6_4

Anatomy of a Sprint

Few things cause more pointless disruption to teams than the fallacy of the two-week Sprint. Even writing this is dangerous. There are legions of agile practitioners and agile desk jockeys who are arbitrarily tied to a two-week delivery cycle. Well, two doesn't mean anything. Why not one, or six? Look at earlier books on agile and you'll see that – as learning to be agile in mindset, practice, and delivery has nothing to do with compressing development and testing into two weeks. Let it go.

Therefore, to make the point, LIFT recommends three weeks or more.

Why three weeks? Three weeks allows organizations that have multiple departments and legacy overhead (again, LIFT is for all teams and companies, not fantasy teams) to coordinate. If your team could really use some extra time for regressions testing, some time to plan the next sprint, and some remediation time, then more than two weeks is needed. I've seen consistent sprint processes of four weeks, six weeks, and two months.

The objective is consistent sprint success and the means to this is consistency and discipline. As of this writing, I've seen the three-week sprint successfully increase quality delivery on at least five occasions, with different teams, different firms, and different cultures.

Consider this scenario:

A financial product that is considered one application by stakeholders (sales, product management, customers), but it's really four different underlying applications stitched together, six services your team maintains for your product, two services you maintain and are shared with other internal teams, consuming three services from other teams, and altogether there are five different databases in play. This is all laid out in Table 4-1. We won't even mention what the infrastructure looks like!

Table 4-1. Dependencies piling up

Dependency	Owner	Quantity
Applications	You	4
Services	You	6
Services (shared)	You	2
Services	Other teams	3
Databases	You	5
	TOTAL	**20**

Some quick math and the team is dealing with 20 dependencies. What is the sense in taking a team that must manage this much complexity and ask them to release new features to production every two weeks? Here are five possible negative outcomes from this setup:

1. Miss on delivery date

2. Miss on scope

3. Miss on quality

4. Miss on planning the next sprint (from exhaustion and time compression)

5. Burns out the team

If you really like two weeks, then go for it. Maybe you have enough release, test, and other automation with verification that the shorter timeline will yield good results. But beware the hamster wheel if you're just getting started. At the end of the day, no one cares. Find the duration that works. You want success – not metrics.

In Figure 4-1 is the anatomy of a three-week sprint. What follows the chart are the important activities across the weeks.

S-0 Sprint Start (development)	(development)	S+3 Test Writing Complete	(dev + test)	(dev + test)
S+6 Mid-Sprint Review	(dev + test)	(dev + test)	R-5 Release Prep Meeting (dev + test)	S+10 R-4 Code Complete
S-5 Pre-Planning Sprint Goal and Story/Slice Candidates (Must Fix Standup)	(Must Fix Standup)	S-3 Retro Planning & Estimating R-1 Release Sign-Off Meeting	R-0 Release (demos)	S-1 Tasking Test Case Writing Sprint Prep

Figure 4-1. Anatomy of a three-week sprint

How to read the three-week anatomy:

S stands for Sprint. So, S+3 is 3 days after the start of the sprint.

R stands for Release. Therefore, R-1 means 1 day before Release.

Week 1

The first week is about making active, meaningful headway on the most important development stories loaded up from planning. Table 4-2 below shows planning for Week 1 happens during Week 3, so don't worry if it doesn't make sense yet. The overall goal of Week 1 is to develop functional software and attack the hardest problems.

Table 4-2. *Week 1 Activities*

Activity	Description
Sprint Start (Sprint Start – 0 days)	This is the rocket launch.
Development + Test	Attack the most complex stories first, in the simplest steel thread approach possible.
	Always do the tough ones first. There is plenty of research out there on why finishing the difficult things in life before the easy breeds consecutive success.
Test Writing Complete	The great majority of test cases are documented by now. These could be in document form, in the work items, or another tool. This is a team choice. (Prefer to include them in the original work item when possible.)
	Maybe you have a test case management tool – hooray!

Week 2

When moving into Week 2, expect to start really closing stories, getting test signoff on important items, and starting to think about the release. The Release Prep Meeting is more important than it may sound. It's doubtful it sounds advantageous at all – well think again. This session surfaces the details that can completely derail a release. If there is one place an engineering team gets slammed by its stakeholders it's botched releases – don't be that team. Table 4-3 belows outlines the Week 2 activities.

Table 4-3. *Week 2 Activities*

Activity	Description
Mid-Sprint Review	This is an opportunity to review all the work completed so far – development, test cases, functioning software, automated tests. Look at the plan and see where the sprint is compared to where you are expected to be. Did the Big Rocks get attended to? Is there complexity left for the end? If so, this is the place to identify these and adjust.
Release Prep Meeting	Start planning for what a release looks like. Are there database schema changes... how will this be handled? Does the security team need to review some new components? Any changes required to the deployment script? Will a new feature need to be flagged on/off and who will do this? Use this time to capture the variables that go into a successful release, plan for it, highlight risks, and find solutions.
Code Complete	Complete writing new software and make final commits! (They aren't final/final because we have other activities like test/fix in Week 3.)

Week 3

The third week is really about Week 1. Yep, now we are planning to start again, fixing must-have defects for the release, and physically releasing the software. Some of the planning activities listed in Table 4-4 can be combined as well. For instance, some teams do not do the Tasking session because the maturity of the team only needs the Planning & Estimating – then when the sprint starts, they naturally order and execute the most difficult work first. Make sure engineers are driving this decision and not project managers, product managers, or scrum masters. Engineers build the software, therefore order the work.

Table 4-4. Week 3 Activities

Activity	Description
Pre-Planning (Sprint Goal and Story Slices)	Planning is a legitimate, organized, controlled activity. This is the session before Planning to pull in outstanding issues, tech design, dependency changes, etc. that should be included in the upcoming planning session. This is not an all-team activity.
	Identify the goal for the next sprint. Look at what you want to accomplish and see if you can slice it up into something that makes sense. But don't worry about it being perfect.
Must-fix Standup	There is a ton of testing going on right now. The must-fix standup includes only items that must be fixed to deliver on the goals of the release. Nothing more. Nothing less.
Retrospective (Retro)	The Retrospective is any format the team chooses to reflect on the sprint, what worked, what didn't. There are many options out there to choose from to run this session.
Planning & Estimating	Planning is taking the work that is targeted to be built and released, discuss it, estimate it, sequence it, and generally create the overall plan for the next sprint. Final story slices happen here. This is usually an all-team activity.
Release Sign Off	Someone from each function (engineering, test and product) gets together and reviews what is in pre-prod, and only then agree to do a release. To make this nice and tidy, document the decision and stick it online where everyone can find it later.
Release	Deploy the software and make it available for your users! Woo!
Task Writing	Take the Plan (from Planning and Estimating) and start to break it down into smaller tasks for the first week of the sprint. This helps everyone understand their role and maximize contributions as the team starts running at S-0 again. (Task writing can be optional and some teams do not like to go to this level.)
Test Case Writing	Write the major test cases, create placeholders for the big rocks, and activate the part of the cycle that makes sure we handle risk.
Sprint Prep – Gap Day	Breathe. Take a break. Clean up code, whiteboard ideas, and prepare for the next sprint. Don't underestimate the impact of a good gap day(s) on prevented burnout and increasing cohesiveness of a team.

Most Software...

Most software looks like Figure 4-2.

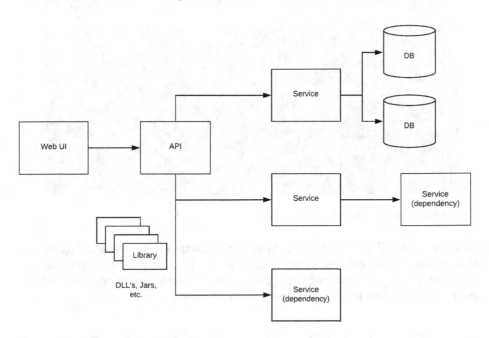

Figure 4-2. Most software looks like this

Sure, your system doesn't look exactly like this. But if you're inclined to read a book about software systems it may not be too far off. You wouldn't be reading this unless there was something you knew could be done to increase your speed, quality, or efficiency. Add in some more APIs, increase the number of databases, include complexity in stored procedures or some other open-source java libraries, etc., and you can make the mental match to your day-to-day reality. There are innumerable variations out there in the details – but business applications follow patterns. Lots of services, few services, thick clients, thin clients – there is not much new under the sun until quantum computing takes off. And if that happens, then hopefully we don't need these books anymore.

Your product is not a snowflake. Your team is not a snowflake. Understanding this will give you freedom to focus on what matters – shipping software.

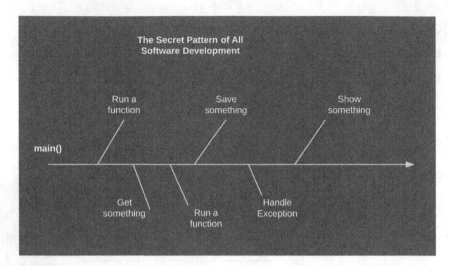

Figure 4-3. *The secret pattern of all software*

Does it matter if most software (business software) is similar like Figure 4-3 above? Yes. 100% yes! The similarities allow LIFT to work. There are only so many technologies, architectures, and dependencies out there and pulling your view up a few levels will allow you to see the pattern.

Non-Functional Requirements Pay the Bills

As software professionals, we aren't paid to solve business problems. That's just nostalgia from mainframe days. Old stuff you'd read in Peopleware or books leading into the turn of the century talk about "solving the problems of the business." Right. That's quaint.

We are paid to handle the complexity, connect the components, enable UIs, secure data, integrate systems, and deliver functionality that in turn incrementally puts the product and business in a position to grow. What is built must work across devices and oceans. It must be superquick and everything that uses a mouse or a tap to navigate is compared to Google Maps or an iPhone.

How do we know this profession isn't all business "problem solvers"? It's so obvious you'll miss it if you don't look hard. Global outsourced software development. We don't outsource, offshore, nearshore to solve business problems. We do it to produce working software.

Produce Working Software and then trust that the product solves the problems set out by the product, leadership, and marketing teams. Working software to Product and Sales teams really means software that runs all the time, quickly, and as expected or better. Working Software to engineering teams can be inspected, debugged, observed, changed, and operated.

Non-Functional Areas to Completely Own

What does it mean to own these areas? It means professionally making sure that the areas receive attention and are included in the build and construction of software.

The key non-functional topics for the BUILD evolution of LIFT:

1. Defensive programming

2. Heavy logging

3. Debuggable software

4. Performance

Defensive Programming

Write code expecting it to fail. Amateurs write software for happy paths. Professionals write software expecting it to fail. Professionals limit hubris and know they aren't omniscient. Expect your code to fail, software to fail, dependencies to fail, systems to fail, and servers to fail. Don't have servers? No problem. Your serverless functions can also fail for many reasons – like network or permissions.

So, how do you program defensively? There are two primary ways: exception handling and guard statements.

Exception handling, for simplicity's sake, in languages like Java and C# are try/catch statements which you can see in Table 4-5.

Table 4-5. Exception Handling

Basic Exception Handling

```
try{
   callSomeRiskyMethod();
}
catch(Exception e){
   log(e);
   doSomethingElseMaybe();
}
```

Assuming you are a full-time programmer or have been a programmer at some point in your career, this looks trivial. You may even be wondering how something so simplistic would make it into any modern book on software. Well, building software is about a strong foundation and working its way up the stack. Is your exception handling really handling exceptions?

Take these steps:

- Have code reviews check for exception handling.
- Is the handling doing what it needs to do?
- Who is taking responsibility? It shouldn't be a manager – look for a respected lead engineer/senior engineer who will put a flag in the ground for quality.

Next up are **guard statements**, which are on a level field with exception handling. In fact, more so for the operations of a working system. While good exception handling will allow software to avoid "blue screening"[*] and crashing, proper guard statements make sure that the execution of code routines is accurate. See an example of this in Table 4-6.

Table 4-6. Guard Statements

Guard Statements
| ```
//EXAMPLE 1
//classic check for null reference exception
if(accountBalanceObj == null){
  getFreshAccountObject(currentId);
}
else{
  //continue execution
}
//EXAMPLE 2
//Checking for a value that affects calculations
if(accountBalance > MAX_CORP_BALANCE){
  return(MAX_BAL_EXCEEDED);
}
``` |

Software engineers can practically end the world by not checking for null! Imagine how many code errors are caught while engineers are debugging during initial development. Do you have that mental picture? Now consider how much slips through the cracks! Checking for null is the easiest way to protect against both inaccurate data and preventing exceptions from bubbling up and crashing methods, routines, executions, services, and systems overall. LIFT is a system and systems include basics. Check for null.

---

[*] This is a reference Microsoft Windows system crash resulting in a blue screen and memory dump.
```

The second example is focused on accuracy. In this scenario, when an account balance exceeds the predetermined amount, the function returns with that error code. The snippet doesn't say what happened before or after and for these purposes it doesn't matter. Protecting the accuracy of the business logic is what matters. In this case, the method returns. In other cases, the code may assign a tracker variable a value and that variable makes it all the way down to the end of the method. There is a time and place for both approaches – and any other of myriad approaches. Don't judge the examples, mind the principle it exposes.

Guard against conditions that will make the correctness of the program fail. This will prevent defects, yes. It can also help to limit inconsistent errors in a system which are exponentially expensive to find and fix. Building software in LIFT focuses on producing working software.

Hello, customer service...

Have you ever been on the phone with customer support, and the agent has a long pause followed by some keys clicking, a sigh, and "sorry, my computer isn't working?" Guess what? That software, built by a software engineering team, has a severe bug. And that bug is causing broader issues than anyone can readily see.

Aggressive Logging

Log like your life depends on it. Seriously – take it seriously! Imagine the derisive laughter of the team taking over after your departure when they tell their product managers the fixed runtime issues software you build because they added logging statements and then read them! Use this as motivation not to be remembered as a hack.

The old team didn't log anything

New Senior Engineer Paul: "Hey, Sanjida (the product manager), guess what. We added logging in the last sprint and see that the shipping routine loops 5000 extra times because of some bug! We fixed it and without even performance testing it can say it's going to free up cycles for customers."

Sanjida (PM): "Really? That's great, the last team just said it was slow because it was old code. Why didn't the last team add logging?"

Paul: "Hmm. Well, I don't want to throw anyone under the bus... maybe they were busy?"

Sanjida: "Lazy?"

Paul: "Yeah. Probably."

Being lazy isn't professional. It's an embarrassment. Here are five reasons to log aggressively:

1. It's easy to log.

2. It lets operators and others observe the runtime of a system with little effort.

3. Developers can get details out of their code at a scale that's not possible in local development.

4. Having log statements allows DevOps/secops/it-ops to construct other systems to make sense of logs, like alerts and events.

5. Logging is the simplest way to pull data out of a system with very little investment.

Questioning logging vs. some other grand idea is excellent in theory. But why push against a technique so well understood and adopted? There are plenty of other challenges during BUILD without sweating something like this.

To continue keeping it simple, log these five pieces of information, and your ops team will high-five you:

1. Log every successful login or failure with an encrypted user ID, date stamp, and user type.

2. Log messages from exception handling blocks that you didn't expect to hit.

3. Log messages from exception handling blocks that you've designated as problematic but expected.

4. Use log levels, info, warn, error, fail, etc. Keep them consistent.

5. All network connection timeouts get logged.

What do you get from this effort? Your operations team can operate the system without calling you and engineering and generating product incident alerts. And as you look down that list, really consider the consequence of #5. Teams can be at odds between "code vs. network" issues. Log the network failures, and there is less to fight about, and you'll help the network team get to the bottom of the problems faster and solve for everyone. Win-win.

Debuggable Software

Software is incredibly complex. Debugging software is a primary activity of software engineers today and far into the future. Therefore, reducing the debugging effort on the software you and your team write pays itself today in both the short term and the long term. After all, as soon as the code ships it's legacy. Someone, maybe you, will debug it shortly.

There is much literature out there on writing debuggable software. For LIFT, focus on these three areas:

1. Small functions

2. Loose coupling

3. Code comments

These three areas aren't going to make the cover of your favorite programming website. They are the meat and potatoes of system engineering and lean towards making software work in small increments while thinking about the end state vs. being a hot trend technology.

> A complex system, contrary to what people believe, does not require complicated systems and regulations and intricate policies. The simpler, the better. Complications lead to multiplicative chains of unanticipated effects. Because of opacity, an intervention leads to unforeseen consequences, followed by apologies about the "unforeseen" aspect of the consequences, then to another intervention to correct the secondary effects, leading to an explosive series of branching "unforeseen" responses, each one worse than the preceding one.
>
> —Nassim Nicholas Taleb, *Antifragile*

Small Functions

Write your functions small, as in short, so you don't end up with spaghetti code, like in Table 4-7 below. It's that simple. No fancy refactoring or software patterns are required to do this, so even the junior engineer can contribute on day one. Functions call functions. Methods call methods. Rinse and repeat.

Table 4-7. *Small functions*

Small Functions

```
Main() {
    getCurrentId();
    getSystemObject();
    log("complete")
}
private int getCurrentId(){
    //call db
    // return id
    //catch exceptions
/* This is considered a short method. */
}
private int getSystemObject(){
    obj system = caller.System.Context.Call.Current;
    return system;
/* This is considered a short method. */
}
```

Avoid Coupling Components

Loosely coupled software components are the second key in debuggable software. It's a term that's thrown around at times by know-it-alls, newbies, or management. Still, it's a valid design concern and one that can assist with debugging software, so should be respected.

The concept is simple, but hard in execution for new software engineers. Don't let the internals of Component A know Component B's internals. You can see this concept illustrated in Figure 4-4. This goes into all kinds of design thinking around abstraction, interfaces, and polymorphic behavior – but don't worry about that yet. Just stick with A doesn't know how B works. A only knows how to work with B – but not what B does internally. This is accomplished differently depending on the language in use. In Java, this is usually an interface or abstract class. It's also achievable via naming conventions and data hiding in just about any language.

What Coupling Looks Like

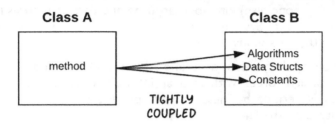

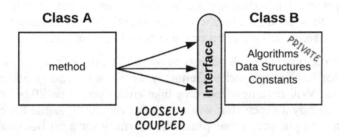

Figure 4-4. Loose coupling of components

Anti-Corruption Layers

If there is one practice that can easily, and I mean quickly, be picked up by even an average experience development team, it's the concept of anti-corruption layers published by Eric Evans in his book *Domain Driven Design*. Domain Driven Design (DDD) approaches software projects by thinking, modeling, and building around the domain using abstractions that work. This is different than the traditional object-oriented programming approach to model the real world with software. As we all now know, an e-commerce shopping cart doesn't mimic the shopping cart in your local Walmart store well at all. Software is nuanced and complex; a shopping cart made of metal is as simple as it gets.

Would you like the benefits of micro-service and distributed architectures like resilience, independent versioning, and deployment velocity without rewriting your world to micro-services?

Well, you're in luck, because the anti-corruption layer acts as a facade or intermediary between System A and System B. It translates what comes out of System B (someone else) into your language and data structures in System A (you). This prevents System B from leaking into your system, and that is more amazing than it sounds.

From experience, all systems, data, and APIs that aren't under your direct control are foreign forces with unclear intentions. That's right. Managing dependencies is serious business as your product's health and long-term maintainability is on the line.

Think of it like this: if you integrate the Foo API and your app breaks or is slow, it's your fault. However, The Foo API team has no problems. They are the service provider, and you are the user. Sure, the service provider has different stressors (reliability, uptime, versioning, etc.), but your failure is not their failure. Your product's loss is your product's failure. Period. So, protect yourself because, in software, no one will come to save you.

Is an anti-corruption layer this additional work? Yes, of course, it's extra work. But it pays for itself very quickly. Generally, in life, if it's too good to be true, it probably is. Will that new exercise bike make you lose 20lbs? Not right away. Can you buy a stock that will surely deliver 300% gains? Probably not. So, you'll have to put your inner pessimist on mute for a bit because creating an anti-corruption layer to protect your system from another team's system will return significant gains. And it will produce those gains almost overnight.

Consider System A (e.g., your system/product/app/service) is responsible for calculating car leases' historical prices. For this to work, A must call into APIs from System B, which return the last three years' costs at different fidelity levels for all vehicles manufactured and headquartered in Europe. They produce data structures ABC, which have GUIDs (globally unique identifiers). This is not unusual, nor is it a problem.

Look at Table 4-8 – System A also has to integrate with System C, a daily FTP drop of 5-year prices for all vehicles manufactured and headquartered in Japan. This integration has yet another data structure and because they are sane, use an increasing numeric value as their identifier.

Table 4-8. Systems at play

System B API – Europe	System C FTP Drop – Japan
GUIDs	Numeric Identifiers
JSON	CSV

You are at a crossroads. Do you want your development team leaking System B GUIDs and System C numeric identifiers down into all your app code? Do you want your junior engineer to understand these two data sources' internals and intricacy and then start coupling external GUIDs to your internal models?

Thus, the creation of the anti-corruption layer.

All the code goes into this layer. This layer maintains the contracts with the other systems, performs data translation, and maps your internal models. The internals of System A now work with the anti-corruption layer, and it can't break. It's your model to your model. Not your model to N models. And there aren't foreign abstractions spreading across your codebase. See Figure 4-5.

If this interests you, please read more about Domain Driven Design in Eric Evans' book. It's also a prevalent practice, and a quick Google search will yield more than enough results to get started.

Anti-Corruption Layer Diagram

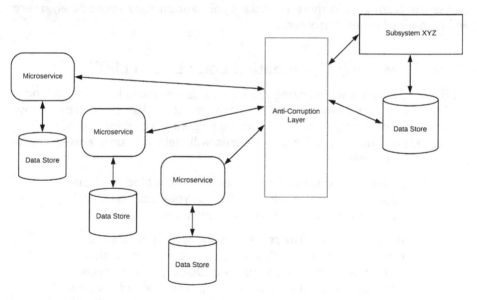

Figure 4-5. Anti-corruption layer working with services

Performance

This is a two-edged sword.

One edge says not to overoptimize, which can also be used to mean don't optimize early. New engineers and those who lack humility throw around old Donald Knuth quotes like "Premature optimization is the root of all evil."

Really? I doubt it.

Let's dispel the misinterpretations of this quote first. He said optimizing algorithms by nitpicking at code before it was profiled was a waste of time. He wasn't saying that optimizing software before it fell over under use was a waste of time.

Take this to its logical conclusion and optimizing the right things early is a healthy practice. Consider a system that handles ecommerce orders – what if it couldn't handle more than three concurrent orders? That's not helpful. Or a system that exchanges records with a regulatory authority. It can handle one transaction a second and then the business development team hits it's goals and sells 100 more licenses. Now, this is not going to be pretty, because unless the team gets in there to make significant changes immediately, there will be a lot of upset customers.

What Does Early Optimization Look Like in LIFT?

Optimizing early means covering the items that are most likely to have non-trivial consequences. Notice this list doesn't mention data structures – those are a topic once the significant items in the following are addressed. Identifying and addressing this short list of concerns will yield less problems over the lifetime of the system.

1. Make sure **connection pooling** is enabled to your database. This will alleviate half of your concerns with adding additional users to your software.

2. Avoid tying **session state** in your web application to a particular server. Putting state in a cookie or a shared system is very easy nowadays. Don't put the session information in memory on your app server. Why? Because when you add another app server, the system will fail behind that load balance as the user state on server A isn't available when the load balancer sends them to server B.

3. Avoid **nested looping**. This one can go under debuggable software, but it's more interesting here because the consequence can manifest itself in the performance of an application. New hire hero developers love to come in and unnest loops removing thousands or tens of thousands of unneeded loops. Keep in mind that processor cores still treat loops in about the same manner.

4. Put guard statements and timers on all **external dependency** calls. For instance, if the application is calling out to a third-party pricing service, the response time is now up to (a) internal queuing mechanisms and thread availability, (b) the Internet, and (c) the service provider's ability. Service providers have bad days, and they release bugs just like the rest of us.

Now, let's consider the other edge of this sword. This side denounces optimizing for scale as not necessary. For instance, internal IT systems really don't need your 95th percentile scale qualities. These systems are usually fixed. A fixed number of internal users, a fixed number of transactions, average order volume, etc.

A few years ago, I ran into a team building a website where the year over year user growth had declined for five straight years. They debated pointlessly on how the system can go from handling 2M unique daily users to 4M daily users. What for? It's not going to happen. It wasn't even the goal of the business! The product team was generating additional revenue by increased annual subscription rates and additional site advertising. In the end, the team delivered a good solution, but it was only for vanity. And the additional complexity will haunt the engineers who one day take over.

Performance is a key non-functional topic because performance needs management one way or another. It either needs to get addressed for scalable support in system design driven by requirements or it needs to be addressed by requirements so that additional scale and performance is not required. Ignoring performance expectations is not a professional option in a world where most software solutions are delivered over the Internet.

Your Definition of Done

Consider for a moment, in your current environment, what does it mean for a story (some work item/task) to be complete? Really, when is the work done? Not ready for testing, not prepared to be committed to source control, not when it's ready for UAT. When is the work item "done-done"?

Having this criterion puts you ahead of many other teams in the industry, so be glad. Don't worry if you don't have this defined – it's one of the easiest things you can do – it will allow you to move faster with more confidence.

Table 4-9 gives the LIFT basic definition of done.

Table 4-9. Definition of Done – Overall

LIFT Definition of Done (DoD)
1. Code has been peer-reviewed and approved by at least one reviewer.
2. Developer and tester have done a walkthrough – risks and scope.
3. Confirmed with the tester.
4. QA performed and issues resolved.
5. Automated tests locally and in the integration environment are green.
6. The story is deployable.
7. Code is finalized for our standards.
8. SQL deployable and tested.
9. All files and configuration changes captured.
10. Product owner signed off on the work item.

Let's do a quick walkthrough of each step. All the steps preferably happen in a non-local environment, meaning the code was committed and in some dev or continuous integration environment.

Code has been peer-reviewed and approved by at least one reviewer.

When Rebecca completes writing her code, she submits a pull request with a code review for someone else on the immediate team to look. The reviewer is looking for functional correctness, possible defects, and any outstanding style issues.

Developer and tester have done a walkthrough – risks and scope.

Assign a tester to every story in the iteration, which, by default, means there are one developer and one tester per story.

QA performed, and issues resolved.

The tester has tested the story using the test criteria and other non-functional and functional criteria required for the product. No issues reported, or issues reported and then retested and resolved.

Automated tests locally and in the integration environment are green.

All test automation for the component/system/product runs locally and in the integration environment with positive (green) passing results.

If a particular story is put into the integration environment and passes its criteria, but other tests fail simultaneously, the story has failed. At this point, the build broke, and the team must fix it. The other tests may have failed from another developer's submission, a network timeout, or other reasons. Test failure is often a point of frustration for a developer submitting a story that they know works. Still - it is the best way forward because it keeps the entire system in sync: it all works, or it's all broken. This binary state allows engineering to be confident in either state.

The story is deployable.

There is a difference between releasing a story and deploying it. Releasing a story means that we have put it into a destination environment of our choice and confirm that someone can use it. It doesn't mean it was successful! That's because stories in professional environments have dependencies. There are three items to cover: the deployment process can deploy the story to a target environment.

First, the code has met the standards set forth by the team. This is knocked out in step 1 of the DoD.

Second, any database changes required for the code to work are deployed into the target environment and tested. Why? Because a missing stored procedure will fail the code.

Third and last, make configuration changes required for the story to function in the target environment. Think of this as anything stored in configuration files/databases/systems. For instance, if this story's function requires a key's value set to "true" in the config file, make sure this configuration gets deployed.

The product owner signed off on the work item.

Finally, we arrive at a sign-off. Let the product owner review the work in the target environment, and when they feel good about it, they will give it a thumbs up. LIFT isn't concerned with formally capturing this decision, but your team can do it however you choose.

Write Things Down and Document As You Go

No two teams are the same, and different teams, even inside the same company, are going to operate at different maturity levels when it comes to documenting and understanding the system. Now, there is no argument that the best way to understand a software system is to write readable code. But is that enough? OK, now toss in unit tests that describe the behavior and test the code, is that now enough?

Of course not. Why?

Because we live in the real world and not some academic textbook or idealized scrum fantasy where everyone does everything, knows everything, has the same desires, and can live via tribal knowledge. Teams are spread out with people in different offices, work from home, and time zones. Information must be documented. And, as we've pointed out over and over, software systems are more than the code. If the build environments, deployment environments, database schemas, and terraform scripts aren't documented in some form, then how will the team ever find efficiencies?

Document as you go.

Eliminate Waste

The concept of waste is highly subjective. The Product Manager may say that waste is any work that is built but not released. The operations engineer thinks it's waste to conduct long releases and manual configuration. And, finally, the software engineer thinks it's all the meetings. Table 4-10 below lists a few different views of waste. So, what is waste?

Table 4-10. *An assortment of beliefs*

	Product Manager	Operations Engineer	Software Engineer
Waste	Unreleased Software	Long Releases	Meetings

Beliefs

It's all waste when looked at from a given perspective. But turn the view, and you'll see just how subjective these concepts are.

The Product Manager needs those meetings because she doesn't know if the development team understands the requirements and sequencing. So, this is how it's done in her world. The Software Engineer doesn't choose to avoid big releases because Operations hasn't worked with them to decompose the production infrastructure footprint. And the unreleased software is a fact of life to both Operations and Software engineering because the requirements for them change too often from Product Management.

Now, none of this is true. It's just a perspective. It's no different than Plato and his allegory of the cave.

In this allegory, Plato asks the reader to consider people born and raised in a dark cave, held in place to only face forward. On the other side of a wall are people who carry objects shown as shadows on the far wall from a fire burning in front. The people held captive see the shapes cast by flame and only know these shadows as objects in the world as they have no other experiences.

Next, Plato suggests that one of these people is set free and led up a steep incline out of the cave and into the sun. The sun burns his eyes, and it takes time to make out the shapes of the real world as his brain cannot believe. Given enough time, this individual prefers the outside world's freedom and new reality and returns to the cave to tell the others. Upon return, he can no longer see in the dark, and the captives believe that the outside has ruined his eyes – and therefore, it would be perilous for any of them to venture outside. And they all prefer to stay.

Table 4-11 below lists more examples of possible waste in the product engineering cycle because they do not contribute to the software's construction, delivery, or operation.

Table 4-11. *Some areas of waste or invisible.*

Possible Areas of Waste		
Wait time	**Build times**	**Debugging**
Wrong tools	Meetings	Extra tickets and tasks
Looking for log files	Big change, big release	Not managing configuration in source control

Teams put these possible waste items in place because of previous experiences and a need to stay in the cave. Let's use the example of the meeting again. The Product Manager states she needs the meetings for a few reasons: gather status, take questions, and discuss the next iteration. The engineering team (dev + ops) says this meeting is a waste because they are busy on the current iteration and don't have questions; they want to remain heads down. Their rationale that the meeting is a waste stems from: they are actively working, and switching in and out of development is a waste of time on its own.

Last year was the Product Manager's first proper software assignment with a different development team. The Product Manager did not meet regularly during an iteration with the team and missed several deliveries that year, reflected in her annual review. Her experience tells her that these meetings are critical, and she must *push* the development team. The meetings are her cave and fire – the shadows on the wall are real for her.

The lead developer tries to pull her up and into the light by taking her to coffee and explaining that finishing the iteration is the team's most critical job, and the mid-iteration status meetings can wait. But to the product manager, skipping status meetings is dangerous. Her only experience developing software products failed without meetings. So, the meeting stays on the calendar, and everyone attends, begrudgingly.

This isn't an attack on Product Managers – far from it. Let's look at the lead developer.

She has been shipping software into production environments for ten years. A lot of what she has learned and internalized tells her continually reducing build times will lead to better product outcomes. That may be true to an extent, but there is a point of diminishing returns. She received rewards for reducing massive legacy applications build times from 60 minutes to 10 minutes in her previous role. It was a stated goal from her manager and did make a difference for the firm because that reduction allowed them to bring on additional teams to make changes to this application to help them in the marketplace. In another role, the architect approved of reducing build times as a breakthrough because the firm didn't have any continuous build and integration previously.

In the current team, she and the team spend 20 hours a week trying to take an extra two minutes off an 8-minute build cycle. This building cycle has several dependencies to bring in, tests to run, and a deployment validation cycle. The team is one iteration behind, the PM is stressed, and the lead engineer won't stop this work because this is what she knows. Reducing build times is her cave and her fire.

Neither the mid-iteration status meetings nor the intense build reduction activities help the team ship better software – so they are both wastes. The team must agree on the waste that everyone understands and fits inside of a given context. Table 4-12 displays what the team needs to identify and eliminate.

Table 4-12. Patterns of Waste

Defects	First and foremost, get the features correct and working as expected. Nothing erodes confidence and velocity like excessive defects.
Wait Times	This is the time that a team member spends waiting for another. This could be waiting for acceptance criteria, waiting for testing to finish, waiting for architecture to finish some service, etc.
Excessive Motion	Too much motion in a software team is often manual configurations, by hand deployments, manual testing, or multi-step environment setups.
Overproduction	Overproduction happens when a team creates code and services they do not need yet. It can also encompass overoptimizations, like the data structure hand-built to handle N varieties of widget types when there are only three and have been three for the last 20 years.
Underutilization	Poor utilization will occur when subject matter experts are ignored by clever engineers, QA team members aren't involved in planning, or developers aren't shown the big picture and treated like widgets. There is so much that happens when our people aren't used to their full extent and books are written on this every year.

Deploy

After going through this evolution a couple of times, a team finds its natural rhythm. And underlying the team's rhythm is the constant drumbeat of "checking-build-deploy" of continuous integration. Now, CI is a standard and table stakes operation, but cannot be left out. After each developer code commit (check-in/push) to source control, a build process must kick-off, run any available tests, and deploy the bits to a development environment.

This environment is how the product, QA, and the entire development team see the fruits of everyone's labor and avoids the "works on my workstation" syndrome.

Activities Summary

A number of these activities are to be constructed the first time through the evolution and then used over and over.

- On the first time through evolution, create Sprint duration and lay in sprint calendar timebox activities.
    - If stuck on a two-week concept without success, try the three-week calendar in this chapter.
    - Stick to the activities inside the timebox.
- Address all non-functional requirements, in the same way, each sprint.
- Defensive programming, logging, debuggable applications, and performance.
- Adopt and use anti-corruption layers like your product's life depends on it.
- Adopt and use the LIFT definition of done.
- Document critical architecture, functions, and decisions as you go.
- Deploy to a development environment continuously.
- Eliminate waste. Every set of activities, including these, has waste. It takes some focus and some grit to eliminate the waste, but doing so will save stress, time, and project injury on the backend.

Test

Evolution #3

The Test Evolution creates a structure proving the software empirically works, is accurate, and has an increased chance of meeting a market need. Understand, testing happens all the way to this evolution, but now it kicks up a notch. LIFT wants software going to production to be ready for use by customers – not tested by customers.

Category	Description
Target	A validated increment of working software with objective, validated test results of positive and negative test cases.
Inputs	A working increment of software from a development environment.
	Detailed work items in the WMT with Acceptance Criteria.
	Goals for this increment of software.
Outputs	A version of software ready for Production.
Visibility	Test Cases & Test Results.
	Risk Analysis.
	Exit Criteria.
The Win	You have tested, correct, Working Software in a QA environment ready to move to Production.

© Stephen Rylander 2022
S. Rylander, *Patterns of Software Construction*,
https://doi.org/10.1007/978-1-4842-7936-6_5

The Problem and Possibility

Planning, constructing, building pipelines, and deploying software is a tremendous amount of work, and by the time you get to "testing" the software, you and the team are exhausted. Plus, pressure is constantly mounting to ship, show progress, demo, and meet deadlines you probably didn't agree to.

Additionally, we have confusion around simply what the software is meant to accomplish. It's not unusual for an engineering team not to know the customer: an internal team, a support team, an external team? This is all a recipe for one or more of these:

1. Catastrophe

2. Stress

3. Make-it-up-as-you-go testing

None of these scenarios end with a happy team or customer. The more chaos around what functionality to test and how to test it, spills more oil onto the floor for people to slip around on. Testing software leads to more arguments and discussion inside of a team than in any other part of the engineering process. Why? Because it's not clear what to do and everyone has an opinion. It's easy to blame testing and testers.

What do you really want from QA and testing?

Most people reading this chapter in this book are not QA professionals. The QA professional lives on the fringe of today's modern business software development ecosystem. After all, the coding boot camps of our timeline don't include the outputs of QA engineers. Nor do our universities specialize in software testing, let alone what the industry calls Quality Assurance. Teams can enter testing phases casually and not be clear on their outcomes. Once you are clear on testing outcomes, then the steps fall into place, and friction is reduced.

Possibility

The possibility is simple: The test cycle is clean, consistent, non-duplicative, and removes risk and stress for everyone. To get there, you must imagine a better working process and environment and then take concrete steps to get there.

See, LIFT is not concerned about Quality Assurance certificates. LIFT accounts for testing and getting quality into products and products to customers. Why? Because we want software. Building software, testing software, shipping software, and operating software. Other methodologies in the middle of the development process only serve to distract and disorient the intended results.

Now testing for quality and prescribed function and non-functional characteristics is fundamental. LIFT has you building these characteristics into software from inception with Plan and into Build evolutions. This type of QA is the responsibility of the entire team (engineers, testers, ops, product) with an internal group of people responsible for testing and communicating risk. This group identifies the risk, shares the risk, and may function more in a quality control manner. Any decent leaders want their QA team (a group of testers) to speak up when they see problems with

- Functionality
- Reliability
- Usability

Principles

Five key principles lay the foundation for the Test evolution:

1. Document Test Cases & Acceptance Criteria
2. Maintain Reasonable Non-Functional Requirements
3. Keep the QA environment clean
4. Set and enforce Exit Criteria
5. Start testing before you start testing

We will discuss each of these, along with the supporting activities in the rest of this chapter on Test. The following is a brief rundown of each principle.

Example user story for the following principles: The story adds new multi-currency calculation to a user-entered textbox.

Test Cases

Any given piece of functionality has more than one path for a user (or process, API, etc.) to take. Therefore, any user story needs multiple viewpoints, which make up the test cases.

Example: This requires test cases validating the currencies supported, null, zero, min-max, etc.

Acceptance Criteria

The current king of all test criteria is the vaulted, esteemed, much beloved Acceptance Criteria. Acceptance Criteria is part and parcel with the agile concept of user stories. There is Acceptance Criteria for every story that goes into your WMT and with it, it is impossible to say if the story fits the needs intended.

Example: When a user enters a numeric value in the currency field, the value will automatically be reformatted to the currency set in their user preferences. The currency will be exact to two decimal places.

Keep the QA Environment Clean

This can be rewritten to: you should be able to eat off the QA Environment. The cleanliness of this environment speaks volumes to the team's commitment to make testing successful. Messy data will equal messy, invalid, inconsistent results. And dirty builds and manual configurations lead to more unknowns. If there is one thing you want to control in any experiment, it's the unknowns. And testing is one big experiment full of hypotheses and results. For instance, do not use the development database for the QA app server. Unfortunately, this needs stating.

Set and Enforce Exit Criteria

Going back to the idea of "why am I testing anyway" comes this rough idea of exit criteria. See, it's easy to write some acceptance criteria for this example user story. Then map out some test cases, like null values, gibberish, form validation, etc. Exit criteria is taking all the work items that rolled into QA and setting clear criteria on when the product is good enough to move out of QA.

Not such an easy answer, is it?

Here the team must get specific around defects, product owner decisions, and the non-functional requirements so that everyone knows what done means in QA.

Start Testing Before You Start Testing

This principle means that the build that enters QA can't be "thrown over the wall." The developers must do their best to test at the unit level (function, class, module, API) and have received some early feedback from the product owner and hopefully a QA team member. The code entering can't be littered with small issues as that will consume all the test cycles and everyone loses.

If the team doesn't start feature testing around acceptance criteria and non-functional requirements before you start QA testing, the likelihood for failure goes up dramatically.

The Testing System

The diagram in Figure 5-1 shows testing starting before entering a QA environment. This is the world's most straightforward development and test cycle. Code, commit, review the commit, deploy to a development environment, and run automated tests. For some teams, if they implemented only this cycle right now (Figure 5-1), their ROI from reading this far is complete.

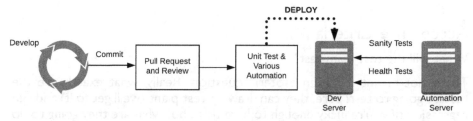

Figure 5-1. Testing that is being done in development and coming into QA

The Testing System is composed of processes and activities, just like PLAN and BUILD. As we know, every system has a beginning and end, so we want to start there. We're going to get into details on all of these, including the practices inside the activities. To begin, in Figure 5-2 is the high-level sequence of activities making up TEST.

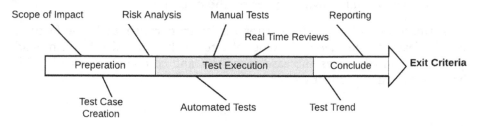

Figure 5-2. *Steps inside of the QA environment and exit criteria*

You'll look at this and maybe think "that's a lot of steps," and like everything in software, it is. It's challenging, detailed, and time-consuming work. Now it's clear though.

For software to get to production in a state that works well, you'll have to walk a journey. And even if you decide you don't want to spend this much time in TEST, these activities aren't going away. What you now have here is a clear sequencing of the activities for success. Let's get into them.

Activities

Prerequisites

To make things simple, most of the prerequisites for testing activities are outcomes from PLAN and BUILD since LIFT is evolutionary, building on previous evolutions. Still, there are some immediate needs that we will double-check here.

Acceptance Criteria

What will the test team test?

That's not meant to be an esoteric question. Really, what exactly are the testers going to test? Sure, they can draw up test plans (we'll get to it) and run regression (if you're lucky enough to have this), but what are they going to do during this iteration? Where does the direction come from?

It comes from the Acceptance Criteria (AC) specified in the work item in your Work Item Management Tool! Every work item (e.g., story, tasks) needs AC so that

1. The developer has a target for what she is developing

2. The tester has a target for what they are testing

3. The product owner agrees on the outcome

Thus, the beauty of acceptance criteria is its tri-purpose: build the feature, test the feature, and validate it. Once the tester has the AC, they can build upon that, add test cases, increase specificity, and communicate clearly with the developer and product owner.

A Build

Stating the obvious is preferred to omitting a requirement, so here it is. The Test evolution needs a new build of the software in their environment. The need for this software is then laid out further in the next pre-requirement, *Environment Entry*.

Environment Entry

To maintain your sanity and to provide clarity to the test team, you'll need to erect some guardrails around changing the QA environment. Why? Because if team members are testing in the QA environment on build 12.3.2 and then build 12.3.3 is released over the top of it, the consequences could be

1. Features under test suddenly change

2. Functionality supporting features change

3. Dependencies supporting functionality, supporting features change

Basically, changing the test environment without the express permission of those testing can generate a cascading chain of events that won't end well.

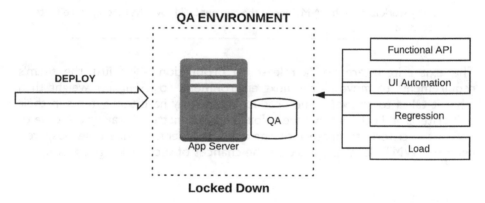

Figure 5-3. QA Environments

Figure 5-3 introduces an ideal state. QA is locked down, meaning that it can only be changed with expressed acceptance from the testers. You may ask if this could be a regularly scheduled event, and the answer is yes, but know that scheduling deployments only builds rigidity and non-required wait times into the process. The best time to deploy to QA is when a round of testing is finished, or something is so broken that the testers want a new build as soon as something is deployable.

The QA environment is then used to test with all the vigor and energy possible. This is where we push automated tests against the UI, deep functional tests against APIs and endpoints, run load and performance tests, and wrap it all up with regression test suites.

All other early-stage testing should be happening in the development integration environment via automated means.

Exit Criteria

The last pre-requirement to enter the Test System is a common, documented, set of exit criteria. The exit criteria are the rules and covenants laid out describing the events and successes required to move the build of software in QA to the next environment in the chain.

Exit criteria is very subjective to the product being built and the team doing the work. For instance, a team could have exit criteria like the following table for a basic stock trading application.

Order	Criteria
1	All automated functional tests against the UI and Core trade types passed.
2	There are no new WARN or ERROR messages in the logs.
3	Every work item in the WMT and in the current build have their Acceptance Criteria accepted.

The exit criteria are not a release to production – it's just the team's requirements to move to the next environment, so it's lighter weight than what it takes to go live. Some product teams may have three items in their exit criteria and others may have a dozen – what matters is taking the time to define the criteria to protect the next environment, reduce false positives, keep the WMT clean, and increase the chances of success for going live.

Preparation

It will require some upfront work to get into the execution part of TEST. Here, there are three activities: Scope of Impact, Test Case Preparation, and Risk Analysis. These activities are a good example of actions that can be performed at the same time as development and deliver the overall effect onto the release.

Scope of Impact (SOI)

We look at the total impact of the changes to the system and from there identify how wide the effects may reach (Figure 5-4). Think of it like an explosion with a blast radius. For a small explosion, the radius maybe 10 feet. But for a large device, the radius may be 100 ft, and as we know, an explosive used in combat could be exponentially more.

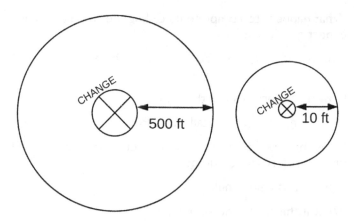

Figure 5-4. Scope of Impact

That is what changing code and configuration can do – ripple out and blast away dependencies and functionality without intention.

Wondering what this means? Let's look at an example.

The purple team needs to change the Pricing API for iteration 24. There are about a dozen work items in the iteration composed of small updates, some configuration from the security team, and two of the work items reflect adding a field to the API output. For context, the API has eight different end points.

Work items were written a few weeks ago as the timing of this change is important for customers, so the Acceptance Criteria is present. For the most part, the values from this new field show up in four places in the product. However, pricing data from this API is displayed in 32 different locations across multiple screens, front-end components, and services. Pricing is displayed to three different types of users: public, logged-in, and paid users.

The question is, what is the blast radius of making this change?

Right away, there are questions like the following that may or may not have been in the AC:

- Is this data point only for paid users?

- Is the data point then hidden for non-paid users? Or is it never mentioned?

- What about free users? Geez, do we have a matrix? Who has this?

- What happens to components calling the API that expect the new field?

- What happens to components calling the API that do not expect a new field?

- Can we identify and be sure that there are only 32 locations showing pricing data?

- How many services call this API?

- How many source files call this API?

- Does the new field add to the execution time of the API or network response time?

- What if this field is null?

- What if this field is non-numeric?

- Will all the web applications that comprise the product need updating?

- Can we change that old enterprise Spring 1.0 Java app that also shows pricing for internal custom support?

So, in this example (see Figure 5-5) the Scope of Impact (with the keyword being *"impact"*) is growing. At first, it's just a new field to an API response. As a developer, this is a trivial change and callers should not care. But just because a calling app should not care doesn't mean there isn't a needle in that haystack that will break when it receives 11 fields instead of 10. And, as the exploration continues, the team sees the full scope across many applications, services, and scenarios which can affect functional and non-functional requirements.

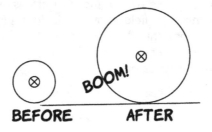

Figure 5-5. A small change ends up having a large impact

Checklist of SOI:

- Where is the change in the software, module, component, API, service, database, network?

- What is dependent on the item undergoing change.

- Will the change alter existing functionality?

- Will the change affect performance? Throughput or response time?

- Will the change alter security or user management?

- Will the change hinder other user functionality, roles, or internal processes?

Scope can get out of hand...

Performing the SOI analysis can help identify issues with the acceptance criteria (not enough), the feature, or sometimes even the general request. Let's use the preceding case some more. Pretend that this new field for the API was to be retrieved from another system. And this system was external to the team's Pricing API. Wow. Now, the impact has just doubled or tripled and the security team, infrastructure team, devops team, and possibly legal need to get involved.

Remember... what looks small can eventually, through some analysis, turn out to be very large.

Test Case Preparation

Test cases are not scary. They are highly repeatable documents mapped to Acceptance Criteria and existing known paths in the software. The QA world has its own language and LIFT neither tries to rewrite this language nor does it actively try to adopt it. Instead, LIFT is concerned with common sense approaches to testing so that teams have what they need to succeed.

Test Cases commonly come from one of these two places:

1. Someone writes Test Cases with the iteration based on the Acceptance Criteria from a work item. Why? Because the AC is the blueprint, and the Test Case is the objective schematic plus an explanation of how the testers will perform testing.

2. A bunch (anywhere from 10 to 1000) of test cases exist and came with the team you have recently inherited or joined. Where this came from is a mystery that doesn't need solving.

As shown in Figure 5-6, when the work item has AC, someone can write test cases off that AC. So, if the work item doesn't have AC, then it's not testable. If it's not testable, why are we working on it. And if this is really the case, it's your job to make a stink about the situation until it's resolved. It is not professional to release software that is not testable. Just stop and figure it out with the team.

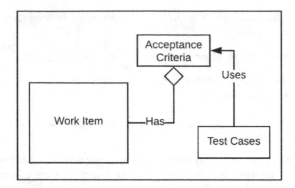

Figure 5-6. Work items and criteria

Write test cases as documents, wiki pages, somewhere in your WMT, or best yet, in a test case management tool. All in all, getting the test cases detailed out in a wiki and linking it in the work item is a rather efficient scenario. But if you are moving towards the need for test suites (which is just a fancy way of discussing an ordered grouping of multiple test cases) you'll want a tool. Still, for LIFT, pickup whatever works (Google Docs, wiki, etc.) and use it until it doesn't work anymore.

A test case contains, at a minimum, the criteria in Table 5-1.

Table 5-1. Test case minimums

Item	Details
Preconditions	The conditions in the system that must be true to move into the test.
List of Steps	A detailed list of repeatable steps.
Expected Results	What is expected to happen after each step, after the conclusion of all the stops, and often what we expect not to happen.
	Positive results. Negative results.
Effort	Just like a development story, how much effort will it take to excuse this test case and a collection of test cases that comprise a feature.
Priorities	Some test cases are more important than others, so make prioritization clear to create efficiency in the system.

This is all well and good and it's clear from the criteria that testing a feature is repeatable and consistent. Now let's look at one test case example based on our fictional Pricing API change. This test case is all contained on one page, but this could change depending on your existing systems. Don't have a test case management tool? No problem, then do the one pager wherever you write documents or keep a wiki.

Test Case

Test Case ID: PRICE-23	**Product**: Kinesis Finance App
Work Item: 52619	**Functional Area**: Pricing
Effort: 16 hours	**Priority**: High

Summary and Notes

Verify that the new field from the PricingAPI, called "Trend" is displayed on the home screen for logged-in, paid users.

Note: we will need to have test cases that cover the matrix provided by the Product Owner for the three user types: public, registered-logged-in, paid-logged-in. Also, make sure we have test cases that cover our full security types.

The AC is in the work item and makes sense to build this test case.

Pre-conditions

1. The current user is logged in and flagged as a paid user.
2. On the home screen.
3. The feature flag is toggled on to return this field.

Steps	Expected Results
1. Navigate to the homepage.	The homepage shows up for a public user.
2. Click login.	Login widget appears.
3. Go through login steps (known).	Success.
4. Return to homepage.	--
5. Look at the pricing component on the right side of the screen. Verify that the field "Trend" is present.	Trend has a value. Any value.
6. Verify Trend is numerical and not-null.	The Trend field is in the table for each security in the list and is greater than numerical, greater than 1 and not null/empty.
7. Manually call Pricing API with security ID and check that the Trend there matches what is on screen.	
8. Refresh the screen and perform step 6 again.	

The test case is now complete to test a logged-in, paid user to see the new API field. The test steps describe the manual process that a human being performs. This doesn't always scale. It sometimes does, if the functionality is more complex to build than to perform, or if the test isn't required often. The industry and you need more of this work automated, scripted, and programmed. The good news is that this test case is easily transferred into an automated test case – each step here maps to some function or process an automated tester or developer on the team can write up. And like a few other topics we've touched on, this is a massive area, and we won't get into many more details on how to automate a test case. Just automated whenever you can.

Test Automation Anti-Pattern

It sounds abundantly simple to automate test cases. You know, just "automate" it. But what does that mean?

For the last twenty years, this means writing code to test your code. In some cases, the tool for doing the automation records the application and is generating code on the backend to re-run it, so more code.

Or teams have been sucked into the UI automation rabbit hole. There are a whole bunch of open source and commercial products in this category, but we will just pick on one: Selenium. You can write a ton of code to walk through and exercise your UIs. Beware, because

UIs change

Tests break

And this is a costly scenario. A very costly scenario. Each time a UI changes, the tests must be updated. And the developer of the UI change has to move around a bunch of hidden HTML tags so that Selenium code can catch it. See, tools like Selenium need assistance to know what to do, navigate a browser's DOM, and clock the right elements. There is no magic.

But what if the Selenium code isn't very good? What if the programmer of the code is just learning how to write test software or it's a byproduct of some other initiative? What if the amount of code it takes to test the change requires more maintenance than the feature itself? Unless the feature is mission critical or safety critical (think healthcare) the return on investment is negative.

Writing more and more code to test more and more code is an explosively expensive situation. The team won't realize the consequences in the checkbook, they will realize the pain via a decrease in velocity and slowing of feature releases and big fixes. Then later, the accountants will shut it down.

Risk Analysis

Looking at the Scope-of-Impact and the test cases we have, what is the risk that these changes will

- Not deliver on time
- Fail testing
- Cause production incidents
- Affect users or systems negatively
- Open other risks through dependencies
- Fail a security audit

The Scope-of-Impact on this work showed a large area of scope and possibly significant impact in several places that aren't changed or tested often. Without even writing more test cases (including the one earlier in this chapter) the QA team members note there are at least another couple dozen test cases for the website alone. Baking in a guesstimate for the other services, screens, and internal tools affected and the number of test cases nears 50.

Communicate the Risk of a given work item or feature to the development team, other testers, and product managers using the following matrix. Every work item receives a Risk Level, and you should expect most to be "Standard" level. An iteration or release loading up with numerous Explosive or Flammable items is a clear indicator of danger.

Imagine a stack of boxes at your front door. Now imagine them again but on half the boxes put Hazmat stickers – worried? You should be, that's why we measure risk.

Risk	Description
Explosive	This is the highest, most critical risk level. The feature could explode and cause damage around the feature's intention.
Flammable	This second-tier risk level means that the feature could cause some significant issues but is solvable.
Standard	The lowest risk level indicates there is nothing unusual about this item.

Risk Analysis is about getting ahead of pitfalls and failure points. The process moves feature development and testing from chaotic to organized and from macroscopic to microscopic. Do not leave details to accident; instead, design the software, features, test cases, and test plans for success up front through thorough test plans.

Execution

Now you're ready to execute. You enter this phase of Testing ready with:

Acceptance Criteria	A Build	Environment Entry and Exit Criteria
Scope of Impact	Test Cases	Risk Analysis

The preparation work is paying off already because you can start testing with a level of confidence. Before we get after it, please remember that these tests are not Unit Tests. Those were accomplished by the software developers during development cycles. Unit test coverage doesn't enter this conversation – everything here is around integration and functional tests, for example, software testing software, not code testing code. This distinction is critical to avoid conflict and confusion.

LIFT TEST is about software testing software, not code testing code.

Automated

It's the year 2021 at the time of writing and most of the test cases brought to this phase are implemented with software automation. There are still manual cases in most business software, and we will cover that a little later. The work now is all "doing," meaning that it's putting hands to keyboards, running through scenarios, and gathering feedback from other testers, subject matter experts, and software developers.

Automating a test case means:

Implementing the testing scenario such that the computer performs the activity and captures the results.

In business software, there are only two major scenarios you'll have to deal with:

1. Testing a user interface
2. Testing the backend of a system (which maybe the entire system, e.g., sans UI)

User Interface Testing

The depth of automated testing is deep. Like, 10,000 Leagues Under the Sea deep, so we must keep this at surface level to avoid drowning the rest of this chapter. Here are the solid options for building automated UI testing (web testing):

1.   Selenium, an open-source framework with much acclaim and adoption, requiring software development in a language like Java or JavaScript

2.   Cucumber, an open-source framework geared towards writing human-readable acceptance tests

3.   Watir, based on the Ruby and back-ended with Selenium

4.   Modern UI adaptation with Machine Learning and AI like Mabl or RainforestQA

The choice is very subjective. The best LIFT can offer for a recommendation are its principles: simplicity, consistency, repeatability. Use these principles when reviewing and choosing a tool to assist you in execution.

API and Backend Testing

The world of API and backend testing is broader than UI testing, but the choice of one tool over the other is not as severe. Here are three tools that can fit the bill any day of the week:

1.   SoapUI from SmartBear Software

2.   JMeter, an open-source favorite for performance and load testing

3.   Postman, which is the current reigning champion of API development and testing

Use the same principles when choosing an API testing tool as choosing a UI testing tool. Each of these three tools brings something unique to bear and each will help you succeed. So don't overanalyze – try two and keep one. Accomplish this objective by timeboxing the activity to two weeks and have the testers do the selection work. Once the testers have selected their preferred tool, bring it to the developers and get their support. Why? Because API testing often needs to get pushed left towards development, so the developers must be comfortable using the tool.

The purpose of testing is to ship software, not to generate QA reports or discuss IIST, CSQM, or any other QA purpose-built acronym. Shipping software that works is what matters.

Manual

Performing manual tests is OK. No matter what you've read or heard from peers, doing some manual testing is not an issue. Why? Because the world is messy!

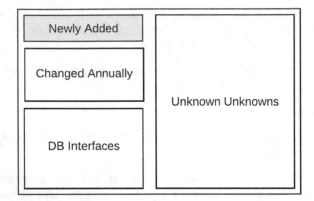

Figure 5-7. Net total code in the system

Figure 5-7 is a 10K foot view of a 10-year-old home builder's item management system. This builder is required to keep track of all building materials used, their manufacturer, those items' source of origin and the blueprints/plans they are associated with. The box in gray is some new code the team added to support building some modern home prefabricated inventory – basically, hold inventory from another supplier before it comes to job sites but will never enter physical inventory. The team added a new API interchange from this item management system to the new vendor to accomplish the functionality.

Then there is another handful of user modules and code that everyone knows changes annually as some relationships change and material manifests improve. And next are a significant amount of database interfaces, because, like so much business software, version one was a direct connection of user interface to database and grew from there. Finally, there is the box on the right – unknown unknowns, which is a fancy way of saying "everything else."

The team has two developers in Ohio, three developers in Mumbai, two QA testers also in Mumbai, and a subject matter expert from accounting in Ohio. No single individual on the team was present when the system was built, and the longest tenure is five years. The chance of inheriting a system with even 30% UI or API test coverage is close to zero. It's not bad or good, it's just the truth.

Therefore, the team is changing about 10% of the overall system annually and currently adding an overall 5% net new set of code for the new feature. They cannot reasonably write test automation over the entire system with the team size they have. However, they can write their new test cases with automation software and keep regression testing the rest manually.

And this is the trick: automate aggressively on the new features and cover the old, slow changing features with manually executed test cases. Eventually, you'll make changes to the slow changing pieces and can write the test coverage with automation. Or, frankly, probably not. Those slow features will not change and when they do, it will be a blue-moon effort and possibly still not worth the time to automate.

Automation is happier with friends because automated tests build up into test suites and groups of test suites yield power of known knowns. Keep moving to exponentially grow automated test coverage and the manual testing won't really matter.

■ **Anti-Pattern Warning: We can't automate that**   Do not let old-timers (long tenure) on a team convince you as a leader on what tests can or can't be automated. For instance, if someone says: that function cannot be automated (coverage with an automated test case) then investigate that. Why are they saying this? Is there a technical hurdle? Is there a knowledge gap? Skill gap? Attitude gap?

The only time not to move towards the automation of test cases is if the effort is prohibitively expensive or won't have a net positive return on investment.

Realtime Reviews

Significant activity happens during the execution phase of Test as there is also development activity concurrently. Realtime Reviews is more a strategy than an activity, as you'll see. As the tester is writing the code for the automated test case (or performing the manual test run for the test case), check in with the product manager. That's it.

Have the product manager review the testing progress, see if the outcomes of the tests really align with her acceptance criteria. Help the tester refine or broaden test case criteria so the results are more expressive, purposeful, or lending to a broader strategy.

Review the progress of testing and test cases with the product manager and other testers.

Conclude

You reached the end of this evolution! All the test planning paid off and the test execution went well. You have automated the new test cases and kept an eye on the old test cases requiring some manual execution of updates. Now is the time to see what happened.

Test Summary and Reporting

The goal here is to identify and share the minimum amount of data from testing required to adjust and judge the direction of the project. For example, which way is the wind blowing – out to calm waters or towards the jagged inland rocks?

To conclude testing, you first need the following raw data set:

- Total # defects found

- Defects found with critical risk

- Total # new test cases created

- Total # tests run

- Total # of tests cases to execute

Then use these to draw the trends in some type of visual format (line charts are simple):

- Defect Rate per iteration/release

- Test runs

- Pass/Fail rate of tests

And finally, summarize all of this for easy consumption by anyone on the team and a sufficiently technical stakeholder with:

- #Manual vs. #Automated Tests

- Test Type #'s for API, Data, and UI tests

- Summarize and then narrate the trend in words, for example, did these iterations' results look better (more efficient, higher success rate, etc.) compared to previous iterations?

Here is an example of it all rolled together. Notice this is focused on easy-to-understand numbers that the team can then use to make changes with.

Testing Summary

Iteration: 23

Product: Kinesis Finance App

Features Planned: 5

Test Cases Created: 12

Tests Runs: 57

Test Cases to Execute: 89

Defects

Total Found	8
Total Critical	1
Defect Running Total	34

Summary

The quality judged by the number of found defects in this iteration improved on what we saw in the past two iterations. Additionally, we made up for the test run gap by executing more of our planned automated tests cases.

This sprint, we still had 20 manual test runs and totaled 37 automated. This means we added seven new automated tests which is the trend we want.

About 65% of the overall test runs were on API, a few on data, and the remaining on the UI.

The team thinks we could plan a couple of those manual test cases to automated conversion next sprint and we are requesting allocation time for this.

Trends

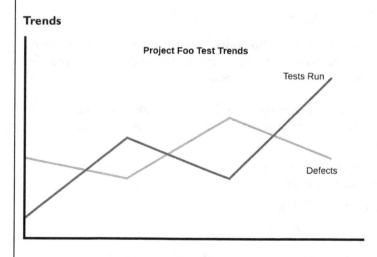

What we discussed previously is the preferred output to the testing evolution. There are times when a team's Testing and writing ability just isn't strong enough to provide the narration. When that happens, and you need something even simpler, use the following template. This doesn't provide the level of detail preferred to adjust, but it doesn't keep transparency high.

Description	Value	Findings
# Features Planned	5	Four of the features released to production. The last feature is still in testing and not needed in prod for another month.
Test Cases Ran – Manual	20	All manual test cases were run.
Test Cases – Automated	37	98.3% of all test runs passed. The remaining were verified by QA/Dev/PM as good-to-go.

Performance

To avoid ad hominem assaults caused by preference, LIFT is concerned about performance, but not for most teams. Only a mature team can take on performance, so, if your team can achieve the TEST evolution, along with the other five evolutions, then performance testing is on the table. If not, the focus should be on progression, continuous improvement, organization, discipline, and details.

Activities Summary

A number of these activities are to be constructed the first time through the evolution and then used over and over. Pay special attention to the Test System – Preparation, Execution, and Conclude.

- On the first time through the Evolution, take time to understand and communicate the Test System to team members
- Next, run through all the Prerequisites and make sure you have them, or define them now:
  - Acceptance Criteria for all Work Items
  - A Build in the QA environment
  - Clear Exit Criteria (governance that allows the build to leave QA for another environment)

- Prepare
  - Scope of Impact
  - Test case preparation and writing
  - Risk Analysis
- Execute
  - Build and run automated tests using test cases covering the UI, API, and data if required
  - Perform manual tests and capture results
- Conclude
  - Double check the stories with passing test cases; also pass the Exit Criteria to promote the build
  - Generate end of testing report; include test trends

Release

Evolution #4

The hard work of planning, building, and testing an increment of software is now complete – it's time to release it! The Release evolution pushes the new software from your pre-production environment to production and available for customers to use. This is accomplished using the tested software and then applying some lightweight release activities to it. These are not difficult; they are easy steps like using a checklist, communicating during the release, and validating functionality at the end of the deployment. Using this sequence of activities means that everyone knows what to expect every time.

Category	Description
Target	Customers can use the new version of software in the production environment.
Inputs	1. A working increment of software from the test environment
	2. List of known issues
Outputs	1. Software in Production
	2. Ignition Launch document
Visibility	1. Release checklist
	2. Release activity play-by-play
	3. Production system validation
	4. Monitoring Systems
The Win	The software is in production, passing all automated tests and/or manual validation, and is clear on all monitoring systems.

© Stephen Rylander 2022
S. Rylander, *Patterns of Software Construction*,
https://doi.org/10.1007/978-1-4842-7936-6_6

The Problem and Possibility

Releasing software is riddled with complexity and unexpected consequences. It requires many people in many roles and doesn't usually end with smiling team members.

Problem #1 – The Act of Releasing Software Is Chaotic

Have you ever had a team of exhausted engineers, testers, operators, and product managers at the end of a release? I have. And many, many teams across our industry have, so if you've not you are either (1) in no need of help or (2) lying to yourself. Because so many teams' releases are chaos.

Well, maybe the act of getting the software physically moved to production isn't always an issue, but everything after that. The question is: what happens next? Just walk away. Have someone "login and validate"? Seriously, this is 2021, and that is so 2001.

I assert that releasing software for some teams is so stressful, so chaotic, so full of dread that people burn out just from this last step. And this is a savage shame, because the act of releasing does not return value anywhere like the creation of new features does.

Problem #2 – You Lack a System to Predictably Deliver Solid Releases to Customers

Your people aren't burned out from software releases? Well, excellent, you're winning. But it's still messy? It still takes more time than is intended and generates excessive noise in the teams and stakeholders. How about the notification that you send out saying "The Foo Bar System will be unavailable between 9 and 10 PM ET for maintenance"?

We all know there isn't any maintenance! You're releasing software and it's unpredictable because you don't have a system. Again, not stressful out of the gate, but that's because the team is masking it by buying chunks of downtime every month. This too is not sustainable. Just wait until the FooBar System needs to be integrated with SalesForce and it can't go down. Then what? A two-hour "maintenance" window?

And frankly, what the heck is software "maintenance"? Software doesn't need an oil change, or its tires rotated, so this is all just a friendly lie we tell ourselves.

Now that you know these problems, let's look at some of the possibilities on the other side.

Possibility #1 – You Let Go of OK and Move to Great

For years, you've probably suffered from awful on one end and merely acceptable releases on the other. The nights of running database scripts, deploying some code, and then trying to test it all. Everything on this scale is mediocre.

This is what we call OK.

The possibility is great releases. And what contributes to a great release? You know exactly what is going to move to production, how it will work, have a plan if it fails, full visibility of the process, and most importantly, feel confident.

Yes, feel. This feeling of confidence is not false or invented – it's present from the work completed.

Possibility #2 – Releases Are Non-Events

Think about it. So many software releases are full of stress and mishaps. But why? Software teams spend weeks, months, or sometimes years to build a new increment of software... and then the most important piece, deploying it to run for customers to generate revenue, and the whole stinking thing falls apart.

Really. It's a disgrace. Thousands of human hours of planning, managing, coding, testing, and configuring and then the release is coordinated the day before and goes off like rollerblading downstairs – just ridiculous and bordering unprofessional.

Imagine if the release were just the last step. Another part of the development cycle that was planned thoughtfully, coordinated with vigor, and executed like a code check-in. That's how it could be.

Principles

Three key principles create the foundation for the Release evolution:

1. Write it all down.

2. Rely on automated tests.

3. Not everyone can be in charge.

Write It All Down

Like so many parts of LIFT, this too is straightforward – if you want to get it done, write it down. Consider the analogy with how people use paper-based planners and what happens with the anxiety and stress of a workday. We will use Sarah for our example, so with her, two things happen:

1. When she writes her day's plans down, anxiety (about the future) reduces, because it's clear what the plan is for tomorrow and the day after and, quite possibly, the day after. Are there changes? Yes of course. But she knows what must go and what can stay.

2. Stress (about right now) reduces because it's clear to Sarah what she needs to do now.

How significant are these changes from writing her day down in her planner? Massive. Anxiety and stress are killers! And they run rampant inside of software development and operations teams, so reducing these in any way is an opportunity not to be missed.

But that's not all. See, Sarah will also pick up some of these key characteristics:

1. She's more motivated. Since her mind is clear from the noise, she has focus and this focus is what individuals and businesses want from their team members.

2. She's more positive. If you reduce anxiety about an activity, make the activity easier, and increase motivation, then you would feel better too.

A software release is often like conducting an orchestra – releasing many different parts of a system from the database through the UI – and these take planning. Sarah writes her week down. The conductor has the sheet music and her orchestra positioned. It's all planned and written down.

Rely on Automated Tests

Pretend that you had to calculate your US Federal IRS Tax Return for the year by yourself (maybe you already do.) Now, here are your options:

1. Get out your own spreadsheet or calculator and do all the math across the 20-200 fields you've entered data into. Then take that number and put it in the final box and tell the government this is correct.

2. Or plug all those same numbers into a piece of software that will automatically calculate the final number on your behalf.

OK, all but the masochistic chose option #2. But, for the stubborn among us, let's say you chose option #1. OK, no problem. But we're going to change the input. Now, you must do this same manual calculation for 10 IRS Returns today. And at the end of the month, you will have to do this same calculation for 500 IRS Returns.

At what point will you want to automate the process by letting the machine do the work. Therefore, computers were invented – to "compute" results on our behalf.

Take this reasoning to its logical conclusion and it's clear that manual testing every release is literally insane. It's repeating the same old, decrepit like of thinking that got us in the position where releases fail regularly.

But wait… what about all the testing in the Test Evolution?

Automate. And rely on that automation.

Not Everyone Can Be in Charge

When everyone is in charge, no one is in charge. And this means imminent failure for a release. Imagine this exchange on the night of a release:

> Sarah: "Bill, go ahead and run the DB update scripts."
>
> Kanna: "Sarah, go ahead and run the service deploy."
>
> Project Manager: "What? Which comes first?"

This lack of coordination leads to exponential problems when the situation, like a release, is timeboxed. It comes down to "going off-script," which we will go over later in this chapter.

The Release System

Like everything in Lift, we are dealing with a series of activities which form themselves into systems. Activities into processes, and thus into systems. Figure 6-1 shows the basic left-to-right release system. The system is made up of the following series of activities:

- A document to describe what is in the release
- A checklist of things to check
- A script describing the order of activities during the physical deployment
- The deployment itself
- Validation of the deployment

Combining all these activities constitutes a "release." A "release" is not the act of deploying software; no, that is deployment.

A release includes all the activities to ship an increment of software into production. There are even more parts of some software releases, far beyond the scope of this book, relating to product management, client communication, release notes, and various business processes.

The critical item to remember for this chapter is that a deployment is a physical act of moving software into the production system, and it's part of a release, see Figure 6-1. Think of it like deploying version 2.2 of the Foo Service as part of our release next week.

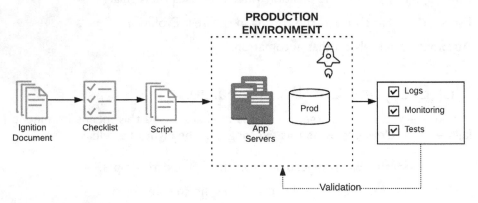

Figure 6-1. Overview of the Release System

Figure 6-1 described the 10K foot view of a release. Figure 6-2 breaks down the activities across three distinct and serial phases: Preparation, Execution, and Validation. This pattern is used over and over in generating processes that fit into systems.

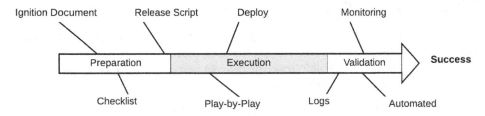

Figure 6-2. *Overview of the Release System*

The preparation phase is critical when preparing a release. Understanding what you have, what you are going to do and having confidence is just as important as automating a physical deployment – or maybe even more so.

Which would you rather have:

1. A house builder shows you their detailed build plan before they start construction.

2. A house builder tells you they will have the house done quickly and don't sweat the details.

A house is a big investment – you want to know there is a plan for it!

A release is not a deployment, rather a release has a deployment.

Activities

Now that you understand what the overview of a release looks like, it's time we dive into the activities.

Ignition

Starting the ignition on a rocket doesn't cause it to lift off the ground. No, instead lighting the ignition gets the rocket primed and ready to launch – the ignition is now on. This is why the name of the initial release document is Ignition.

The Ignition document covers the scope and definition of the upcoming release. These are the sections of the document which we will dive into:

1. Release Summary
2. Release Details
3. Roles
4. Dependencies
5. Risks and Mitigations
6. Release Script
7. Rollback Plan

Release Summary

The release summary is just what it sounds like – an overview of the release.

Maybe you highlight some fundamental changes, or critical risks, or key success criteria. Summarize what is in the release. Please think of this as the elevator pitch you tell the executive when she asks what your team is releasing next month.

Now, you must store and share this document. It doesn't matter if you made the document in Word, Google Docs, or some wiki. There is little value in spending much time on this decision – just use what you have available. Put all your Ignition documents in the same folder structure, in the same place, every single time, and then share this location with everyone. I recommend using a folder structure divided by Product, but you may divide by team or some other arbitrary system. The only thing that matters is consistency.

This is what a release summary looks like:

The goal for the 2.4 SHO release is to get out the new backend APIs with all the security changes from the last audit. This concludes all of that workstream. We also address a number of customer-reported defects.

Release Details

Now that you have the purpose and goals of the release, we can move onto the important information – the details! This section is not subjective or fuzzy – it's the significant, tactical details about the software we are deploying for the release.

Here are the items that go into release details:

- Change List
- Release time and date
- Deployment items
- Other release links (testing plans, load tests, deployment items, etc.)

Change List

A change list is simply a list of work items which are in the latest software build ready for deployment. Remember all those work items planned, built, and tested? It's those. The change list isn't manually created nowadays – just run it all from your WMT (work management tool) and insert the link. If your WMT has nice ways to version your changes, great, use the best tools and features at your disposal.

The Change List answers, "what code changed in this release."

Release Date and Time

This is the date of the release and the time it starts. If you have a window to communicate, OK, but this is just the date and time.

Deployment Items

This section lists the services and apps that are being deployed, since a release typically contains multiple deployable items. Table 6-1 has an example of this case.

Table 6-1. Deployment Items

Deployable	Version	Deploy Notes?
Foo API	2.3	None
Commerce Web App	3.5.23	None
Synch Batch Job	–	Stop the jobs first.

In this case, we are releasing an API, a web app, and some backend batch job. These are clearly listed because the folks doing the deployment need to know what's going on, verify versions, and have the context for their release script.

Other Release-Related Links

This section lets you add in anything else of interest to the deployable items or for the release. Most common are links to executed test plans (as proof that things were tested), load test results (more proof), and any internal company approvals.

If the release has infrastructure or architectural changes, include that as well.

Roles

The introduction to this chapter highlighted chaos as a major problem for software releases. Since releases are organized by people, a lot of the chaos is therefore human-made. The simplest solution to alleviate this problem is to assign roles, as seen in Table 6-2, and put it in the Ignition document.

Table 6-2. The roles of a release

Role	Name
Engineering Lead	A developer from the team who knows the code.
Release Lead	Coordinates deployment activities.
Test Lead	Someone from QA and representing testing during the deployments.
Operational Lead	This person is an SRE, admin, or operational pro.
Performance Lead	Often optional, and focused on measured performance.

Why aren't there responsibilities listed in the table? Because responsibilities are extremely organization specific. LIFT doesn't prescribe organizational structures and titles. The roles are simple enough though and separate from someone's day-to-day role.

For instance, the Release Lead can be anyone. It can be a senior engineer, a QA engineer, a project manager, or maybe someone in your team (company) whose primary full-time responsibility is releasing software. The roles are hats. You wear the hat and then take it off. Other people can wear the hat next time. But two people can't wear one hat. But one person can wear a couple hats in opposition to the analogy. Why? Because LIFT is based on real life, and you may need the same person to be Operational Lead and Performance Lead.

Dependencies

Dependencies are everywhere.

These are all dependencies: database(s), another team's API, your APIs, a third-party component, or an upgraded UI library. In the Build Evolution earlier, we looked at an example team finding they had over twenty dependencies while they thought they only had a small web application. The dependencies section of the Ignition document allows you to list everything you consider a dependency that impacts the deployment or, just generally, affects the operation of your application.

Again, this is nothing fancy, it just gets the information communicated to facilitate other conversations or actions if required. Usually, for Ignition, you can just call out dependencies that are changing. See Table 6-3.

Table 6-3. Dependencies listed in the Ignition document

Dependency	Owner	Notes
Calculation Service	Central Team	They released a new version last month.
Fund Database	You	We are deploying several new stored procedures and one index update.

Wo is to those who ignore their dependencies.

—Anonymous

Risks and Mitigations

A risk is anything your product team considers dangerous or volatile that, if left unattended, has a high probability of derailing your deployment and overall release. A risk is exceedingly contextually specific.

Consider, your new version of software has a new JavaScript library update – a risk for this could be "browser compatibility issues in the wild."

Or maybe the release requires a dependency from another team to be in production before your release – a risk here is "cannot deploy onto the old version of the calculation service."

Risks are great to call out and you'll feel a little relief getting the items that can generate failure recorded with various eyeballs on them. This is not the intent. In business, a risk without a mitigation is worthless.

What is a mitigation? A mitigation is the act of reducing the severity or impact of a given risk. We are just scratching the edges of the broad topic of risk management. What's important to remember is that every listed risk must have a mitigation. If the risk doesn't have a plan to eliminate (to mitigate the risk), then the risks are just a wishy-washy list of complaints – and that helps no one.

Risk, mitigation, risk, mitigation – this is the pattern. Think about it: when Sarah, the senior manager, asks you if there are any risks to the release and you say "yes, lots" …. what do you think she expects from you next? Do you think she will high-five you for creating a list of things that can go wrong? No! She will ask "what are you going to do about them." What is the plan? This is risk mitigation.

Release Script

I will warn you now. This is boring. The release script is the order of events for the deployment. It can be at the 10K foot view or very detailed – this implementation detail is up to you. Often, it's like a Test Case. See Table 6-4. We will get more into this topic later in this chapter, the thing to know is the release script goes into the Ignition document.

Table 6-4. Release Script Introduction

Step #	Action	Executor	Expected Result
1	EXAMPLE: Run Script "foo.sql" in the "/sql/foo" folder.	DBA	The console says, "updated 1 record."
2	Run the web app deployment from Jenkins.	Operational lead	Jenkins console says "success" and the home page comes up.

Rollback Plan

A rollback is the set list of actions to perform when the deployment won't deploy, or the deployed system doesn't work. It's the sad day when you trying to deploy *FooService* v2.0 and nothing works with it. The rollback plan is then all about how to get back to *FooService* v1.9.

This too is a series of steps to take, written simply enough for the Operational Lead to execute with minimum assistance.

The rollback is the step to take when everything fails. It's not a happy day. But if your deployment fails, the systems are not working, the last thing you want is eight hours of downtime while the team figures out what to do in real time.

Ignition Summary

And finally, share the document. Yes, send a link to the document (seriously, don't send copies) out to everyone who needs to know. I've had success posting this to the same instant messaging channel or a consistent "upcoming release"-related email alias that blasts out to interested readers. The point is this document has action items and meaningful information for the release, therefore people need to read it, or at least reference it – so don't hide it.

■ **Note** You may be thinking this sounds old school. Is this really what I want to do? And I agree. But this book exists to shine a light on a vast reality and then move to make that reality easier to manage day to day. We must find success in our current environments before we can make moves towards anything leaner or faster.

Release Checklist

The checklist is as powerful a risk mitigation tool as anything you will find. The checklist is used for everything from "don't forget the milk" to-do's all the way to "this rocket is ready to launch." The inherent efficacy of writing down what needs to be completed in order and then checking them off a list is the way humans control variability and generate safe environments. In the Release evolution, we create a consistent checklist of what needs to be done, each time.

I worked in an industry called EHS (environment, health, and safety) for a short time in my career. We built SaaS software for companies operating with hazardous materials, large mechanicals, or warehouse operations. All these companies have people exposed to risk adverse situations – being crushed, starting fires, or spilling hazardous materials.

For instance, consider an oil refinery. If you've ever seen one, they are a maze of pipes, valves, and switches. To stop the flow of material from one section of pipe is not just pushing a button. There are multiple steps required, in a certain order, to be performed exactly, every time. The consequence of not following the checklist. Explosions, equipment damage, lost time, and bodily injury. Now, if you ran this operation, would you let the team do this type of work without a checklist?

In software, we bypass this all the time. We think Fred has a great devops mindset and skillset and his scripting and deployments will work the same every time and we can trust him.

Trust him? Trust no one. If you only take one thing away from this chapter, please let it be to trust only the process and checklist. People are liabilities. Therefore, we automate testing. Therefore, we write unit tests. Don't get lazy on the last mile of a release.

Are you still not convinced?

NASA deals in nothing by complexity and safety critical systems. This is from the 1990 Paper "Flight-Deck Checklists."

> *Checklists should contain, in abbreviated form, all the information required by the trained flight crew to operate the airplane in most normal and non-normal situations. Normal checklists should be organized by segments of flight. The checklist should contain the minimum 22 cues required for the trained crewmember to verify that the appropriate actions have been completed. Only procedural steps which, if omitted have direct and adverse impact on normal operations, are included. Items annunciated by crew alerting systems are not included.*

> —Flight-Deck Checklists

The authors of this paper are sharing this from another association, the Air Transport Association, who has the same recommended philosophy as airframe manufacturers (think Boeing) and all airlines (think United, Delta). They all agree — a flight crew needs a checklist.

We would not have commercial flights without checklists. Why? Because five percent of planes would have crashed annually during the golden years of air travel, and no one would fly.

And, finally, healthcare. In 2001, critical care specialist Dr Peter Pronovost tried creating a checklist to approve one problem: line infections. He created a checklist of five steps that the practitioner will follow each time they change a line. They then monitored line infections in the department where the checklist was used and, in a year, they saw the ten-day infection rate went from eleven percent to zero. When they extrapolated those numbers out, it predicted they saved two deaths, dozens of infections, and over a million dollars in costs. All, from a checklist.

Release Definition of Done

You now see how powerful checklists are. Here, we are going to focus on a specific type of checklist called the "Release Definition of Done." Those familiar with agile development strategies are familiar with the Definition of Done (DoD) and we outlined this in the Build evolution. This is what it means for a development story to be considered complete. The criterion for done is always more than "I'm doing writing code."

For Release, we've taken this concept and created a Release level DoD. This level allows a cross-functional team to hit all the major actions required for a successful release. See Table 6-5.

Table 6-5. A sample release checklist (APM stands for agile Project Manager)

Item	Eng	APM	QA	Product
Performance and Load Testing				
App Speed and Load Requirements Defined	X			
App Speed Testing Accepted	X		X	
Load Testing Accepted	X		X	
Security				
Application Scans Complete	X		X	
Monitoring				
Checked New Relic	X			
Checked Logentries	X			
Checked Other Logs	X			
Infrastructure				
Network and Cloud Diagram Shared		X	X	
CAB Approval		X		
Operational Readiness				
Regression Tests Completed and Passed			X	
Project Launch Plan Created		X		X
Release Plan Created		X		X
Coordinate with Ops Team	X	X		
Train Customer Support				X
Dependant Partner Signoff		X		X
Communication Plan		X		X

This checklist covers what needs to be done and who is responsible for doing it. This list covers all the major cross-functional areas I've seen across multiple teams and industries in established environments:

- Performance and Load testing
- Security (of course!)
- Monitoring
- Infrastructure
- Operational Readiness

Your requirements might be a little different than this example list – that's not a problem to capture what is most important to you. You can add or subtract from this checklist as needed or move responsibility from one lane to another. Have your agile Project Manager use this checklist to move the release forward daily and share it publicly.

When every item on your Release DoD is checked off, you are ready to deploy the release. This way, it is clear what items are creating risk and everyone is informed.

Release Script

The concept of the release script is like a checklist but sequenced across multiple topics and individual functions. Use the release script for complex releases with multiple moving parts. Meaning, if the release only has a deployment of a single service with minor changes, there isn't a lot of sequencing required and therefore probably won't need a script.

Communication

How are you going to communicate during the deployment and release process? Just choose. Using a conference call, Slack/Teams/Instant Messaging, or email are all acceptable choices. Just choose one and use it every time.

LIFT recommends instant/group messaging because it's real time and standard nowadays.

Create a working agreement on how the deployment communication channels operate. For instance:

- The main channel is for people with a Release Role to communicate about steps in the release.

- Stakeholders can't post to the main channel.

- Questions about the release happen in a separate, named channel.

These are not hard and fast rules, rather they are guidance on the kind of rules required to remove noise during a release.

Play-by-Play

The play-by-play is the detailed deployment script. This is when you list, in detail, the steps to take to achieve moving all your software from a non-production environment to production. The more detailed, the better, because the operator of the deployments won't have to ask as many questions and the deployer role becomes more portable.

Here you list actions, in order, like

1. Shut down all batch jobs on prod-batch-01/2/3/4.

2. Turn off synthetic monitoring.

3. Run the deploy-prod-app job and review output.

4. Etc.

The contents of the play by play are 100% specific to your environments and products.

Fallback vs. Rollback

Part of a deployment is building in plans for the contingency – for example, when things fail. You want to enumerate the steps for the return to a normal running system because some of your deployments will fail – that's just life. The deployment will fail because of a defect, a dependency, or being rejected for some other business impact rationale.

There are two ways to accomplish this activity:.

- Perform a fallback – the return to another copy of the system that is operating concurrently.

- Perform a rollback – the reversing of all changes to a previous version.

Let's talk about this a little more.

Some teams prefer building their systems for a fallback scenario, so they have two production systems, an A and B. A and B are identical infrastructure environments and are interchangeable.

Fallback is going back to a current operational system as the deployment failure strategy. This setup has several advantages, like

- Returning customers to the old software can sometimes just be DNS pointer changes or script execution.

- The change is idempotent and well known.

- Testing is straightforward as the fallback system never changed.

And like everything, there are some disadvantages:

- The cost of purchasing and running duplicate environments

- The cost in time/labor to maintain duplicate environments

So, if cost is not an issue, setting up your environment for fallback is ideal, as you can see in Figure 6-3.

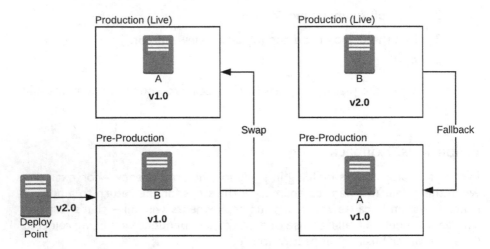

Figure 6-3. A deployment swaps A for B and then a fallback is B back to A

A rollback has the same outcome as a fallback, which is the previous version of software for customers. Executing a rollback is much more intense than a fallback if your environment is more than a single application. You will have to run deployments of the previous version against all destinations and have a strategy for backing out database changes. This is a common, though not recommended, setup, so there is no other guidance to provide here that isn't extremely context specific to your environments.

Production Validation

The software is now in a production system and it's facing customers (with a live deployment) or about to face customers (with an A/B deployment). What's next? Validation.

Logs

LIFT anticipates basic non-functional characteristics like logging – any type of logging. Table 6-6 below lists the places you need logging and thus the logs to check post deployment.

Table 6-6. *Logs to check*

Log Type	Description
Log Tool	This is your log aggregation tool containing access to all the logs that follow.
Application Logs	This is the ideal log to check as it's created by the application at runtime. You may need to check server by server unless you have a log aggregator.
Server Log	This is the log information from a given server's operating system.

Let's say the deployment completed at 9:05 PM CT – then start checking the logs for all events after 9:05 PM CT and keep looking for the next ten minutes. If you don't have natural user traffic during your deployment window, you'll have to generate traffic (see the following text for automated testing). However, having testers (or engineers, or product managers or anyone with a pulse on the release) perform a login, run through some basic scenarios, etc., should trigger log entries into any of the log types mentioned earlier.

You are looking for anomalies, errors, and warnings. And then investigate errors immediately and have someone look at the warnings.

Monitoring and Synthetics

Monitoring… where to start? The entire world wants to talk about the monitoring of systems. Most of us have had some stakeholders ask, "don't you have monitoring?" Well, what does that mean? We'll get into that more in the next evolution. For now, we will pretend we have the items put in place from the Operating Evolution chapter.

After a deployment, check your monitoring tools. That's straightforward… whatever tooling you are using, look at it now. Hopefully you were looking at it during the deployment, but no harm no foul at this point.

You can't see monitoring screens for your products? That's a major smell to address right away.
This means you have either an operational team to talk to or someone hoarding information.
Either way, if you're accountable for the release, you get to see your systems in prod.

Next, as part of monitoring, look at your application synthetic results. These are the real transactions run against your systems using scripts. For instance, "go to homepage, login, verify page past login has XYZ on it." Again, we'll get into more details in the next evolution.

The long and short of checking monitoring first is that you'll see big red flags immediately. Maybe an app server CPU just jumped to 90% or you are losing available memory like crazy. And on the synthetic side, if the tests start failing, you know something is wrong and you can investigate the failures. A release is never over until all monitoring is green! Get to green!

Automated Tests

Continue using your automated tests from QA and Stage/UAT against your now live version of software in production. This requires having a subset of automated tests whose sole purpose is production validation. These fall into two categories:

- Smoke Tests

- Sanity Tests

The smoke tests validate the most basic of functionality, like hitting the applications home page or performing a login. The sanity tests go a step deeper and validates new functionality or bug fixes deployed. Both suites require success to finish the release.

Release Complete

Just like a work item needs a definition of done (from the Build Evolution), the release has criteria we hit to mark the release complete. Once the logs are clear, monitoring is clean, and the automated tests are green, the deployment is complete and the release is done. You are complete!

Activities Summary

To review, a deployment is inside a release and the deployment has a specific sequence of activities. Follow the steps for each activity and a release will become a non-event:

- Review the Principles of a successful release.

- The foremost activity is to create the Ignition document. This document captures a lot of information that is often left unsaid and relegated to tribal knowledge.

  - Change list

  - Release Date

  - Deployable Items

- Roles and Responsibilities
- Dependencies
- Risks and Mitigations
- The Release Script
- A rollback plan

- Modify and use the Release Checklist to ensure step-by-step success.

- Create a release script to keep everyone moving forward during a release and control variability.

- Finally, validate the production release with logs, monitoring, and automated tests.

Operate

Evolution #5

Operating a software system is often taken for granted as a secondary or third level concern when designing and building new software systems. This myopic focus on build and ship, at the expense of quality and operating capabilities, is a key drive for what this book and system are all about. You'll see that operating a system in production is non-trivial but not complex. It too is a series of activities, concerns, and outcomes.

■ **Note** You may already be operating your system, and therefore you are starting this evolution before Plan.

© Stephen Rylander 2022
S. Rylander, *Patterns of Software Construction*,
https://doi.org/10.1007/978-1-4842-7936-6_7

Category	Description
Target	Running the released software in production in a consistent, predictable, and low stress manner.
Inputs	1. A system in production
	2. A team with potential to operate production
Outputs	3. A system of to observe the software
	4. Operating procedures for issues (tech, rotations, post-mortems)
Visibility	5. The internal mechanics of the system in production
	6. Issue lists as they arise and for mitigation later
The Win	You can see issues rising before they become full problems for your systems and customers. Plus, you have a predictable way to handle the situations and control the impending chaos.

The Problem and Possibility

At this point your software is in production and that is something to celebrate. This event also introduces a new set of problems – ones that your current skillsets and capabilities may not be able to address. Let's look.

Problem #1 – You Have No Idea What Your Software Is Doing

The software is shipped – yeah! Now what? How many errors are happening daily on the connection to your internal dependencies? Is the software running as quickly and responding as timeline as expected? Do you even know what is expected for response time?

OK, this is easy stuff. How about the data? Are all your records being saved? Can you prove it? Most of the time teams have no idea if their production software is doing what is expected unless someone complains.

Problem #2 – There Are No Hooks to Observe Internal Behavior

A hook is a method that an external system can connect to and extract relevant information. You don't have anything like this programmatically so it's not possible to, say, have your software call an external API on interesting events. Your software is static, not dynamic, so brittle to change and observation.

Problem #3 – Incidents and Accidents Just Happen with Little to No Consequence

The result of your inaction is telling everyone around you that you just don't care. You and the team are a walking generality with no concept of specifics.

The system is slow.

The page only partially loads.

Records are missing from the database.

A whole segment of customers cannot login.

All these things are incidents in corporate systems and SaaS, yet they just keep happening to your projects and things only improve partially and slowly and no one is ever held accountable.

> The problem is not the problem. The problem is your attitude about the problem.
>
> —Captain Jack Sparrow

Possibility #1 – You Know What Your Software Is Doing

You wake up with confidence your team knows what is going on with your software. You have tooling in place to let you see the transactions and API calls inside your software. You have logging that is active and being used pumping out logs of errors, warnings, and important information. And synthetic key transactions are running against your application consistently, so you know what is happening for customers before issues become incidents. All this tooling is used productively and in a consistent manner.

Possibility #2 – When Incidents Happen You Know What to Do

Oh no, customers on the west coast can't login! Wait, you know what to do. First, internal alerts go out before customers start complaining so the response team is already in communication. The right people are paged, the right data is being reviewed, and communications are flowing. Troubleshooting has started before you even get involved. And, after functionality is restored, the situation is reviewed, items are created to prevent this incident from happening again, and the system progressively becomes more resilient.

Possibility #3 – You Live in a World of Specifics

The entire operational support plan of your software product is driven by data. You know the response time thresholds for all key areas of the application and how many concurrent users it can support and what the requirements for support are.

And it's like this all the way down – from performance to usage to error rates. Customers use the software to solve problems that computers can solve. You live in a world where specifics rule and generalities are slowly turned to data that is actionable.

Principles

Three key principles create the foundation for the Release evolution:

1. Measure Everything.

2. Test Everything.

3. Operating procedures drive change.

Measure Everything

Be specific. Every application, service, and the components that make up a system are made up of attributes that describe the function of that system. Therefore, these applications, services, and components are measurable. Why? Because everything in life is measurable. Table 7-1 gives a few examples.

Table 7-1. Everything in life is measurable

Steps taken daily	Sleep hours	% Carbon in the air
Milligrams of mercury in water	Your dad's age	Your doctor's years of experience
# feathers on a duck	# fishes in a lake	Mb/s download speed

If it's an object, virtual or physical, it has characteristics. These characteristics can be observed and measured. And since we can measure all of these (random) items/concepts, then we can measure the software systems we spend millions of dollars to create and maintain. Table 7-2 below enumerates some of the items we want to measure in our systems.

Table 7-2. *Measure your systems*

# APIs	# API calls/min	#API calls/sec
Most called API	Most visited page	Least visited page
Longest running query	Most used query	Etc.

You can even measure your measurements.

Test Everything

Now, once you can observe and measure the characteristics of a software system, you can test those characteristics for validity or thresholds.

All of this is applying the scientific method to software. This is not a new concept, as nothing in these patterns is new. When characteristics of software are observable, they are measurable. If something is measurable, that means we can run experiments on them – which is what testing is. Testing is what you do to run an experiment and validate (positive or negative) a hypothesis.

Scientific Method

The scientific method is a method to study natural science since the 17th century. It consists of systematic observation, measurement, experimentation while creating and validating a hypothesis.

The next logical step is to form a hypothesis (test cases) and generate experiments (tests) against these characteristics. For instance, here are some basic operational tests:

1. Browse the most visited page in the site.

2. Query that the longest running query is within its measured acceptable range.

3. Perform a browser-based login to validate the login works.

4. Ping each internal API every 5 minutes to verify they are working and responding in a given threshold.

Operating Procedures Drive Change

You see, these principles build on each other and need one another. A software system is measured and then tested – in as many places as needed, for example, test everything everywhere. But this choice of activity isn't random either.

One of our possibilities is to operate in a world of specifics. Therefore, to create this world, we need specific procedures to follow over and over. These repeatable steps produce feedback loops, and this feedback informs the changes to make to the software (code and defects), features, non-functional characteristics, and operational changes to reduce the support required. You must use the same process to generate the feedback loops so that each experiment (test) follows a similar process.

What does this mean?

Consider using a compass in the wild. You are out in some rocky wilderness – hills, rocks, plenty of trees, and your line of site is never more than about 30 yards or so. You need to get back to your camp and know it's west of where you are right now since you hiked east by using your magnetic compass. The surroundings do not look familiar but there is still plenty of daylight. So, you are fairly sure you can navigate back.

Do you:

A) Navigate back using your compass?

B) Throw away the compass and use the sun?

C) Guess which way to walk and start walking quickly to get back before dark?

You use the compass. Why? The operating procedure to return to camp is to head west. And your tool of choice to find west is the compass.

Unfortunately, software and operational teams often wander around or change tools midstream without a real rationale.

If you leave with a compass return with the compass.

Activities

The activities of the Operate Evolution build upon each other and start with an assumption you are new to Operations. The focus is getting a stable foundation by putting consistent procedures in place, create ways to observe the system, and only then start moving towards responding and preventing problems. There are helpful tools which ease the processes that are discussed in this section as well.

Standard Operating Procedures

Imagine you are making spaghetti and meatballs for your family dinner. This sounds simple and you've made it many times and the family has eaten it up. How does this process go? Let's start with the sauce, and you proceed thus:

1. Heat olive oil on medium-low in a large pot for sauce.

2. Chop onions, carrots, and celery.

3. Add vegetables to the pot and let them slowly cook to create the base. (Vegetables sweeten when cooked low and slow).

4. After they are softened, at least 20 minutes, add whole peeled San Marzano tomatoes to the pot, salt, and pepper, increase heat to medium and cover for one hour, stir every 15 minutes to prevent sticking and burning.

   a. If the sauce is starting to burn, reduce heat and add two tablespoons of water.

5. (Abbreviating now) Prepare, form the meatballs, and fry.

   a. If cooking 2 lbs. of meatballs, use two frying pans.

   b. If stovetop is full, bake meatballs at 425 degrees for 25 minutes.

6. Cook the spaghetti in boiling water.

7. Serve.

This is a standard operating procedure. It outlines the procedures to follow to start work and provides guidance on the procedures to then follow when circumstances change – like in step 4a. The goal of writing a standard operating procedure is to create consistency and safety.

Imagine if you didn't have a process to follow when making spaghetti and meatballs and you did it different every time. Putting raw meatballs in a cold pan or adding the raw onions to a completed pot of sauce isn't going to yield the results required. Letting the sauce burn – not so tasty anymore – which means it's not a usable product.

Of course, to create the maximum amount of chaos, make this meal without the instructions and bring in three other team members with their own opinions!

A Standard Operating Procedure is like a recipe with contingencies.

You will have Standard Operating Procedures (SOPs) around anything that is operational. What is considered operational?

Table 7-3 shows many activities and structures which are operational in a software-based system.

Table 7-3. Operational Items (the most important)

Infrastructure management	Monitoring	Tracing
Incident management	Cloud management	Security
Deployments	Build pipelines	Log management

You'll need SOPs that cover what is most important to the release of software and then operating those applications in production. Therefore, to move on the item in Table 7-3, you'll need an SOP for each area. Nine areas are a lot to take on, so here is the minimum set of SOPs you'll need with a focus on working software in production:

1. Deployment SOP

2. Monitoring SOP

3. Incident Management SOP

4. Infrastructure SOP

Now, you can focus on the deployment, monitoring, management of production issues, and the hardware across all your application stack in a concise way.

Here is a partial example of a Deployment SOP:

1. Pull latest build number from Jira build list.

2. Verify build date is within last 24 hours.

    a. If not, email engineering manager for verification.

3. Shutdown the *Foo Service* on Node 1.

4. Run the *deploy.rb* file against the latest build UNC path.

5. Check the Foo logs.

6. ...

A standard operating procedure (SOP) is a set of written procedures or instructions for the completion of a routine task designed to increase consistency, improve efficiency, and ensure quality through systemic homogenization.

The SOP is best written as a checklist, just like we outlined in Evolution #4 while using the checklists for Releases. A release checklist is a type of Standard Operating Procedure, we just hadn't yet defined this construct because it exists much closer to the operation of systems than the development of them.

Create Observability and Monitoring

Now that you have a means to create repeatable operating processes with SOPs, you can put the first few major operational blocks in place. All production (and most non-prod) needs two core operational systems:

1. Observability

2. Monitoring

And, no – these are not the same thing.

Observability is the introspection of running software. We are materially looking inside a running piece of software and the system. For instance, take our favorite, the *Foo Service*. Observing the *Foo Service* includes looking at the *Foo Service* at runtime and application tracing at runtime. The key to observability is looking inside on a running application as it executes to promote active debugging and application understanding. Often, you don't know what you are looking for before observing an application.

Now, monitoring is like observability in that we are gathering data, but it's more focused. Monitoring is the set of tooling and practices to watch a system using a predefined set of metrics and logs. Monitoring shows what happened at the system level by looking at events from an outside perspective.

To better understand these concepts, please refer to Figure 7-1. Here, you can see that the application has many technical stakeholders in its operational footprint.

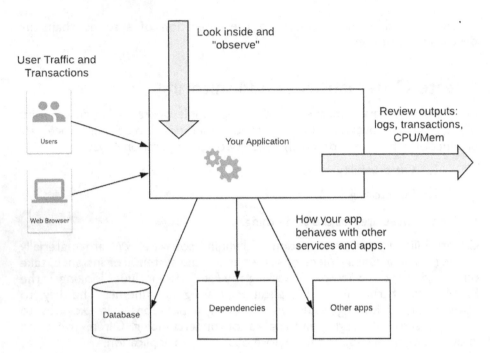

Figure 7-1. The complete view

Let's work left to right across this diagram.

On the far left, labeled stage 1, we have the user inputs into the application: this comes in the form of user interactions (traffic) and transactions they take (search, submit, etc.). These interactions are often captured in a predefined state as usage metrics. These actions kick off most of the application activity in the system.

Next, in the middle, stage 2, is the large application box. The box can stand in for one application, several applications, or an entire sub-system. The application is acted upon by stage 1 user traffic. The application uses other systems as dependencies, generates data for monitoring, and is observable.

In the bottom row, stage 3, are the dependencies of the application. Interaction with these dependencies is a core part of the system (consider how fundamental an application's database is!) and they too generate telemetry events for monitoring or that influence results of observability and application tracing.

Stage 4, the far right, includes all the telemetry, events, logs, and predefined metrics for monitoring that the execution of the application generates. This data is consumed by monitoring tools.

And, finally, stage 5 at the twelve o'clock position of the diagram is the observability functionality looking inside the application at runtime and capturing application tracing and real-time interactions with dependencies.

Operational Tooling

Ah, tooling. We have not talked much about tooling during the last four evolutions, and we won't get into specifics here either. In the following, we cover the types of tools required but do not make recommendations as the breadth of offerings is forever changing.

Figure 7-2 shows your toolbox. You will need something that handles each of these observability and monitoring needs plus some others.

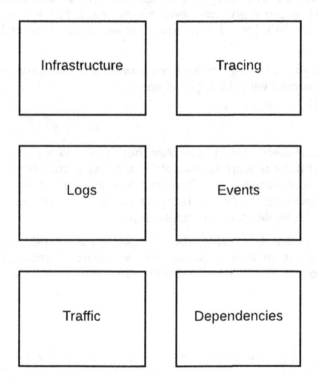

Infrastructure	Tracing
Logs	Events
Traffic	Dependencies

Figure 7-2. Your Toolbox

Infrastructure

This is monitoring tooling for the basics of your environment: server-based CPU, memory, and storage usage. Without a doubt, this is the most basic level of monitoring available.

Logs

You need a log aggregator. Maybe you're thinking, "no, I can just log into machines when we are investigating." The response to this is, you're right. You can also hot wire your car everyday instead of using your keys, but no one does that.

Aggregating (forwarding/copying) log information from all your applications and devices to a single searchable location has immense value and is a reason that the big tool companies in this space have been so incredibly successful over the last 20 years.

For the aggregation of logs to succeed, you will need to give some thought to your log levels. You remember those right? Levels like info, warn, error, critical, etc. Require applications to log with an accurate level so that sorting, filtering and searching at the aggregator level makes sense. For instance, this is a common filter: "All log entries from server name like ordweb* with level=error".

This amounts to: find all log entries from server names that start with *ordweb* and that are marked with the log level error.

Traffic

Where are your users coming from? Are they coming in from a web browser in your office? Remote work locations? Or are they customers connecting to your products over the Internet from locations all over the world. You need a tool that reads user traffic that hits your servers and records their activity in web browsers while using your application.

This data is immensely valuable when deciphering any production problems loading web pages, or slow response time with possible geographical issues. Plus, your product team will learn a lot about their users and customers from the data.

Tracing

Application tracing is the core concern of observability, so consider this your observability tooling. You will need a tool that is currently popularly known as Application Performance Management. There are big players in this space and now many smaller-to-midsize offerings, since it's grown to be such a vital tool for teams who build and operate software on the Internet.

Events

Events are publications of activities of particular interest captured in a central location. It's like log aggregation... but for events.

Want an example of an event?

- CPU exceeding 98% on machine FB89ORD01
- No files received to FTP for more than 25 hours
- Memory running at 50% capacity for more than 2 hours

Dependencies

Modern teams look at their dependencies as much as the software they ship. Why? Because the success of your software is only as good as the software it depends on. The cheeseburger is only as good as the bun, etc. To look at your dependencies, rely on the Tracing and observability tooling – so the Application Performance Management (APM) tool.

Now, you may go and look at adding these tools to your toolbox to find out that event tools or an APM cost money. It's true. LIFT Engineering expects to spend some money at some point. So, here's the thing. If you run a product, like SaaS that generates revenue (and is therefore quite important), then spending money on some tooling to increase revenue won't be a big issue when you work with management.

On the other hand, if your software is internal, you may not get backing to purchase an APM. Do not distress. Internal tools usually don't need deep application tracing because they exist on a different plane than SaaS. For example, you probably don't need it, so you can leverage what your team/company has or get by with a focus on free/OSS log aggregation and monitoring tools.

And, to conclude the tooling section – which tools are a must and a showstopper, shoot-yourself-in-the-foot, not to have?

1. Infrastructure
2. Logging

If you don't have at least these two and your solution has even one dependency (API, DB, other service, external party) then you are just going to have a very hard time executing the Operate evolution. Finally, if you find yourself in a situation with no tooling, no support for tooling, and no budget for tooling – then it's time for you to move on anyway.

Responding to Problems

Production problems are always operational problems, but not all operational problems are production problems.

In this chapter, when we refer to problems, it's an interchangeable terminology with the phrase incident or issue. Some teams say:

"Yeah, we have issues in prod."

While others say: "There is an incident in the live environment."

Or "Prod is having problems right now. Don't even get me started."

They are all referring to things happening in our customer serving environment that we do not want to happen, most likely orbiting around availability, performance, or correctness. For our purposes, we'll use the term incident.

Use Your SOP

We spent a bunch of time earlier in this chapter talking about standard operating procedures. An incident response process is a classic SOP. Write up who you want to do what and when and you'll be miles ahead of where you were.

Restore Service First

Lengthy and intimidating frameworks exist for the prescriptive handling of incidents, resolving them, managing them, tracking them, turning them into problems, and a whole lot of other complicated procedures.

But that hardly matters when there is a problem in prod. Only one thing matters: restore service for customers.

What does this mean?

If the application is slower than usual and not usable, restore it to normal speed. If the application is down, bring it up. If the system is showing incorrect prices, get correct prices in there.

A service, for a customer, is simply any action they are trying to take. And the job of any engineer is to make products work – now.

It's like your electricity. When it's dark and storming and the power goes out, do you care what they must do to bring it back on? Be honest. You don't. Pretend your local power company reverted over to a big pile of burning coal and rubber gloves while they restore parts of the fried electrical towers somewhere. Maybe they come to your block and snake big green lines across the street because the south side of the street has power, but your side was without. It's a temporary solution to the electrical company – and to you "service is restored."

That's it. Restore service.

This is when you're allowed to change production servers and configuration, deploy new code rapidly, take bad servers out of rotation, or reboot that database at 2 PM.

Reliability is a prerequisite to success.

—Anonymous

Respond Only to Synthetic Monitoring Alerts

Synthetic monitoring is recorded (or written scripts) that perform interactions with a (web-based) application using a web browser. To the application, these are real users because they are everything but a human doing the work.

Is this a type of test automation? Sure. Synthetics are operational though and keep an eye on the system from an outside perspective.

In previous chapters, we referred to the Foo Service. We can't test the Foo Service via synthetic monitoring because the Foo Service is internal. Here, we run synthetic scripts against the Reporting Application, which in turn uses the Foo Service (and a dozen other services.)

Our synthetic runs through a web browser on remote infrastructure, usually in some datacenter or cloud-based infrastructure, and then executes the steps in the script through the web browser. The beauty here is your synthetics can run from many different geographies also teasing out other possible production complexities, like slow east coast compared to Midwest transactions.

Your team should only respond to alerts coming from the application itself.

But what about the infrastructure monitoring? Well...if your CPU is running hot but the application is working as expected, does it matter? No, it doesn't. It's not a production incident...it may not even be an issue to investigate unless it begins negatively affecting application usage.

So, don't respond to noise or hunches. Respond to failed synthetic monitoring only. Making this part of your standard operating procedure drives teams creating better and wider sets of synthetic tests and keeps the focus on: Is Production Working as I expect?

Rotations

This is very much based on who is on your team today or your ability to hire new roles. Figure 7-3 shows our example team setup.

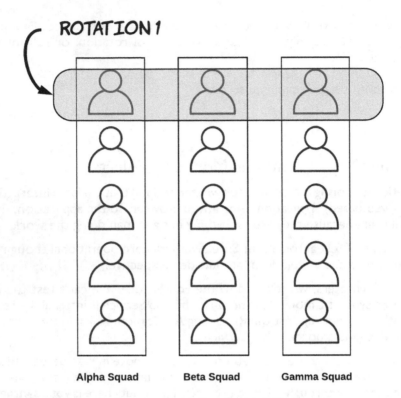

Figure 7-3. Slicing production support rotations from existing teams

The LIFT approach is to take engineers and divide them into rotations or mini "tours of duty." This works best on 1–2-week intervals. If your system has lots of problems, you'll need to stick to one week less your folks burn out.

Here you can see we take slices across teams and put them into a rotation support schedule. Equip them with your SOP on production incidents and let it roll. Feedback comes in from your rotational support team members and improvements are made, rinse, repeat.

Long-Term Fixes and Mitigations

As the team triages and troubleshoots production incidents, they will find a few things:

- Reoccurring issues

- Black swan type of unpredictable issues

- Unreproducible issues

All of these need a mitigation plan.

What is mitigation?

mit-i-ga-tion

the action of reducing the severity, seriousness, or painfulness of something

Any problem you want to go away needs a mitigation strategy. That's it. Find out what it takes to make the problem not appear again and you're set.

Let's look at a few examples.

Example 1 – Reoccurring

Issue: The application is critically slow for the last two days of every month.

Root Cause: Users run end-of-month reports at the same time.

Mitigation: Add application caching for large reporting runs and two new reporting servers.

Example 2 – Unpredictable

Issue: Off-hour pricing updates on the warehouse are no longer finishing by 6 AM CT.

Root cause: The sales team sold 1000 new seat licenses to a large customer in an oppositive team zone. These 1000 new users are overwhelming the system during the hours 1–6 AM CT.

Mitigation: (1) Move pricing calculations up by two hours and add 12 more vCPUs to the cluster to finish before this customer comes online. (2) Setup new communication channels with the sales team to prevent being caught off-guard.

Example 3 – Unreproducible

Issue: At 12:10 PM CT, Monday, all fund prices should "NaN" on the Reporting App. By 12:15 PM CT, all prices were back to normal.

Root cause: Unknown

Mitigation: Unknown. Research continues.

The sum of mitigations is to fix issues before they become major problems by organizing action lists and executing them back in your Plan evolutions.

Anti-Pattern Alert!

Beware of the quick fix becoming part of the cement. The problem with that broken file share permission which blows up the stock pricing on the website is not the permission. It's the dependency. Sure, the permission is what made the file unreadable. But the dependency is what brought pricing down.

Getting to the root of problems is not easy nor obvious. Everyone has to put on their Sherlock Holmes hat and ask what was the problem that caused the problem that caused the problem that caused the problem. Logical deduction and investigation will yield large results.

Why? Because that file permission will eventually break again.

Think about this – should your website (and customers) be dependent on some random, old-school file share between old windows servers? Seriously. No.

The solution is to remove the dependency and replace it with something that is resilient.

Service Level Objectives

As much as LIFT tries to avoid tedious acronyms, we can't avoid them all. Service Levels are a hot topic in the industry and will continue to be as the drive towards SaaS continues and firms rely on myriads of outside applications to run their business. To play this, and it is a game, you must know the basics. Table 7-4 outlines the key topics and definitions.

Table 7-4. Service Level Objectives

Topic	Definition
SLO	Service Level Objective. This is the desired state of any given application, service, or component in the system. This metric is for internal use only.
SLI	Service Level Indicator. The attribute measured to assess conformance to the SLO. For instance, if the SLO is 99.9% availability, then the SLI is the Uptime Metric measured from the monitoring tool of choice.
SLA	Service Level Agreement. A formal, usually contractual, agreement between the provider of a service and a paying customer. For instance, an SLA may include a requirement for 99% uptime and a 24-hour rolling average page response times under five seconds.
Error Budget	The error budget is calculated by measuring the tolerable space between the internal SLO and the contractual SLA. Example: The SLO is 99.9% uptime, and the SLA is 99% uptime. The error budget is .9% of the year, or 78.84 hours. It is normal to have a stricter SLO than SLA so that you can manage the difference. 365 days * 24 hours = 8760 .9% * 8760 = 78.84 hours

OK, great. How do we use this?

Work against your error budget.

In Table 7-4, we see that the Error Budget for the Reporting Application is 78.84 hours. This means that the application can be down for 78.84 hours before we breach the Service Level Agreement. Managing against the error budget thus means we are keeping track of total hours (budget) of downtime as it moves towards the SLA.

The SLI is how the measurement for the SLO (and thus SLA) is measured. In this case, it's uptime. So, there is synthetic monitoring in place checking the application every 5 minutes, 24 hours a day. This metric becomes the Service Level Indicator.

What follows is an awful scenario, but pretend that the year starts and in the middle of January the Reporting Application goes down for two days and a total of 51 hours. Everyone is stressed and working to restore service and bring the system back up. At the end of all this, the database vendor and their premium partners flew in overnight with new boards for the database hardware and did a hot install to bring the system back to life. This is quite an awful scenario, but realistic. By the end of this ordeal, the remaining error budget is 27.84. Eleven more months are left in the year, and you will be in major agreement breach if that application is down for 27.84 hours.

What do you do? Make significant upgrades across the entire stack to help the application stay up for the remainder of the year! There are no tips or tricks for that – it's all specific to your application at that point.

Measuring what you want to achieve is a no-brainer. But doing it is rare for so many teams. When you measure what you want to improve, things will improve – and you'll stay on the good side of your sales partners and customers.

Create Performance and Stability Improvements

Now that you have some idea how and why to manage an error budget and the criticality of setting SLOs, you have a tangible and meaningful mechanism to push performance and stability improvements up the backlog and into planning scenarios.

When the error budget is running low, changes must be made. Wait. They don't have to be made – your company can be OK with being sued for breach of contract written into the SLA, which is often an addendum to a larger contract. Yes, yes, this stuff is boring – but it is the big why to many decisions around operating production systems. Customers don't care how you write your software – but they care if the application they pay for is working when they need it.

Between performance and stability reports from the field generated by the rotating production support team and managing the error budget, there are plenty of items to schedule that will improve performance, stability, or both.

Push this information back to Plan and use the data collected here as evidence. It's your responsibility.

Manage Change

Controlling change is quite simple. It only becomes complex as the number, size, and scope of systems increase. This is then triggered by legacy systems, their replacements, and the technical baggage that follows without retiring old equipment and applications. The following is the most straightforward and efficient way to manage application changes into production environments:

1. Schedule the release.

2. Notify others of the scheduled release.

3. Release.

See, the simplest way to manage change is just to schedule the release. Now, change can come in more flavors. Let's look at some network infrastructure change. This is a good topic because it's the same scenario for a data center or in a public cloud provider:

1. Schedule the network router upgrade.

2. Notify others of the scheduled maintenance.

3. Perform the upgrade.

Wait — isn't that the same series of events? Yes. That is change management for running software systems. Anything else that lands into change management at companies is driven by other internal processes and policies. For instance, your company may have a policy that says network upgrades can only happen during the second week of the month. Or a policy stating full source code security scan completions and review before a release is scheduled. It doesn't change the overall pattern.

Schedule, inform, and perform the action.

Summary

Here are the patterns to learn:

1. Use Standard Operating Procedures to create safe predictability.

2. Getting inside an application is more powerful than observing it's outputs.

3. Measure everything.

Operating production systems is not easy, but it's not complex. Create predictability, use a small set of the best tools you can afford, and make sure your decisions are based on data. With that, you're way ahead of the curve.

Activity Summary

Some of these activities may feel foreign to you and that's OK. The concepts of SLOs, observability, or things like log aggregation used to be strictly in the "operational professional" domain. But times have changed, and all these activities continue to push left towards development cycles.

- Create and use Standard Operating Procedures.

- Create observability and monitoring across your application tiers.

- Keep track and leverage your logs.

- Choose the best tools you can afford that get the job done you need to observe and monitor your systems.

- Create and use incident response processes.

  - Create rotational incident response teams.

  - Restore Service above all else.

- Measure and create SLOs using SLIs that all support your SLAs.

  - Set aggressive SLOs for yourself to promote continuous improvement.

Manage

Evolution #6

Here you are, evolution six of six. You have seen the problems, the possibilities, and the activities to move across planning, building, testing, releasing, and operating your software. Problems like, we live in chaos and possibilities like, repetition of activities builds results.

The Manage evolution focuses on taking repeatable, strategic steps in the management of the entire LIFT Engineering cycle. Each time you complete the six evolutions, it's called a "system cycle." From this vantage, you are looking back down the mountain you've climbed and it's time to consider the things that worked well, the activities to improve on, and the people who helped get this release out the door. Whether the release was the first for a new product or one in a long line of deliveries, the activities are the same, meaningful, and described in this chapter.

> *You can have it all, but you can't do it all.*
>
> —Garrett J. White, founder of Wakeup Warrior

Figure 8-1 shows you are now at the end of the evolutions for this cycle – but the work is not over.

© Stephen Rylander 2022
S. Rylander, *Patterns of Software Construction*,
https://doi.org/10.1007/978-1-4842-7936-6_8

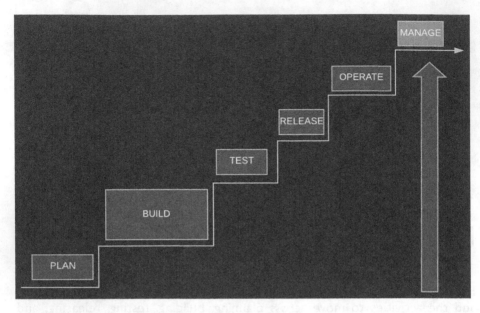

Figure 8-1. Manage is the top of the evolutionary climb

▧ **Note** LIFT Engineering provides the evolutions, which act as the patterns to keep applying to the process. In this evolution you will see how this entire system is self-sufficient to recycle again from the start.

Category	Description
Target	A plan on what to change, improve, or remove in human interactions and events before starting the evolutions over.
Inputs	1. An operable software system in production
	2. A team that has released software and dealt with running their system in production
Outputs	3. Improvements to make across the next completion evolutionary cycle
	4. Reflection points on what did and did not work
Visibility	5. Documented change improvements anywhere across the evolutions
The Win	You (and the team team) are proud of what they shipped to production and prepared to start the evolutions again with confidence.

The Problem and Possibility

Like in each evolution, there are problems to address and possibilities to create. The Management evolution is the only evolution requiring introspection and is the least prescriptive in nature. But make no mistake – skipping this evolution would only hurt adoption of LIFT or any engineering system.

Problem #1 – Now What?

Moving through the evolutions with their activities to land here at the Manage evolution required dedication. The path was simple, yes, but the number of enumerated activities was probably surprising compared to how most practitioners think about building and shipping software. This level of detail is the same result when you take any activity and break it down into its constituent parts.

So, the question is: what do I do now? Do you go back through the evolutions exactly like before? The completion of a long shipment of software is often the time leaders and teams stop. The first problem is what to do next.

Problem #2 – People, People, People

The second problem is people. The LIFT Engineering System provides prescribed and repeatable sets of activities and measurements that lead your team from evolution to evolution. The only consistent factor across all evolutions working towards a shipment of software is people. Seriously – everything else is continuously evolving (code, test plans, deployments) outside of people.

Engineers, testers, product managers, executives, managers, system admins – they are all just people. And people's interpretations, opinions, beliefs, and actions are the only thing separating your software shipments from leveling up.

Possibility #1 – It's Easy to Make Improvements

Improvements are easy to make. The first possibility to create in your mind is improvements are easy. It really is. If you took a team through five evolutions to land here at *Manage,* then you've already learned how vital continuous progress is. Now, you see that making incremental improvements to activities in the system is not only necessary but easy and repeatable.

Possibility #2 – Skillsets and Mindsets Are Adaptable

Your people are upgradeable. That is, everyone has a set of skillsets and mindsets, and these can be trained, grown, or adapted to the goals around LIFT Engineering, the prescribed activities, the skillsets, and the use of guided autonomy to accelerate delivery across each evolution. Your people grow and change, and they must for you to stay consistent (e.g., not slip backwards) and execute at a high level.

Principles

This evolution is based on principles of improvement across the lifecycle of the evolutions.

Evolution Changes You for the Better

Business, which all of software is outside of academics, is loaded with case studies of leaders and high achievers explaining how they achieved their results. There is a common theme. They improved themselves to become a bigger and better version of themselves. This self-improvement allowed them to achieve results as individual contributors or excellent leaders.

Focus on being more, not doing more. This focus of improvement yields exponential results and is directly under your control.

Walk Then Jump

Forget the crawl, walk, run analogy towards learning and maturity. Software teams aren't babies!

Instead, growth from professionals better fits this model:

Take smaller steps,

Take bigger steps,

Jump.

Here, the team is to take more small steps – each Evolution is full of these activities that constitute many small steps. And then take the larger steps – do more, be it iteration and release cycle, by reducing your cycle time and make big steps in quality and reduced timelines.

And finally – jump! Jumping are the big gains that LIFT doesn't even try to cover in our small, repeatable, consistent step-based approach. An example of jumping is replacing architecture A with architecture B. For example, moving a system with database level integrations to a service-based architecture is a jump.

Why? Because we want our professional teams to move faster and with more confidence. Telling a team that it's OK for them to "crawl" at any stage of software construction is insane. If the team has no idea how to build and test software (crawling), you are toast. Don't even bother.

The principle is to build a better you, that makes the team better and then set expectations to change move quickly for everyone else.

▇ Software Is Built by Professionals

Your teams are professionals. Not family or children. Treating them like children will get you the same results as having children. Therefore crawl, walk, run is not the model LIFT uses.

Your Stories Are Currency

Use your experiences to tell experiential stories which demonstrate the principles and practices for the LIFT evolutions. Everyone has stories in the industry of what did and didn't work. Tell these stories. The best speakers in the world tell stories. The best writers in the world tell stories.

When you want to move teams towards peak excellence, step by step, moving towards jumping, tell stories so they are motivated and can visualize change. When people start to visualize, they are becoming active participants.

Everything Is an Action Plan

Show me an object which is completely static, and I'll show you a false dichotomy. Everything on this earth and universe is going through constant transition – only the rate of change differs.

If you can see an object, you can try to change it – but maybe fail at the attempt. However, when you can measure this object first, you'll succeed. The evolutions and activities are all improvable through purposeful action. To create discrete, tangible, action, it requires a small plan. Not a capital "P" plan, like the first evolution – just a little action plan to kick it off. Everything we change requires at least a little plan, and we call these Action Plans.

Why? Because it's more liking calling a play in sports than planning a winning game strategy. There is more to come on this.

Activities

All the following activities are things to do. Even at the manage phase, our principles, thoughts, and retrospectives lead to next actions. What is the problem, why is it a problem, and what is an action to alleviate the problem?

Plan Short and Think Long

Don't let that round of high fives lull you into thinking all is well and good in the world of shipping software. It's not and it never is. There is always a wolf circling your campfire – and it's made up of a hundred little decisions that can throw your entire equilibrium off.

Imagine circus performers spinning plates on the end of long skinny poles. If you've never seen this, it's quite awesome to watch. Now, they don't just spin the plates onto the end of a skinny pole with their hands and then wait for momentum to slow down and fall off.

Why not? Because no one pays to see that. The plate would fall of in about, hmm, seven seconds. They twirl these long poles in such a way that it balances the plates on the ends of them – and they never let the momentum cease. For, as soon as an object loses the minimum velocity to maintain motion what happens? It comes crashing down.

If a bird stops flapping its wings and it runs out of lift under its wings…it crashes. You get it now.

If you let momentum stop, velocity reduces precipitously, and the system will break down. To avoid this, take on an *Improvement Challenge* after each significant release using the document in Figure 8-2.

IMPROVEMENT CHALLENGE

○LIFT

Instructions:
Choose one Evolution to improve on. List the challenges. Then list a new target outcome.

Evolution	Challenges	Target
PLAN		
BUILD		
TEST		
RELEASE		
OPERATE		

Figure 8-2. Use the Improvement Challenge worksheet after every completion evolution

The Improvement Challenge is simple to conceptualize – look back across the last five evolutions, pick an evolution and then choose an activity inside that evolution which was challenging. In your first couple go-arounds, this will be easy to spot. It's only when you're maturing that the improvement areas require some searching. Using a preset document template to facilitate the improvement challenge simplifies things and brings team members onboard quickly because of its visual nature.

Here are a few ways to use the Improvement Challenge document:

1. As the leader, you can choose the challenge and new target yourself. Then let the team know.

2. Distribute the document to each team member and have them fill it out and review the submissions as a group.

3. Set up a short (like 20 minutes!) workshop with the team and choose the challenge together.

Or make up a different flavor. Just because we list vanilla, chocolate, and strawberry doesn't mean you can't choose mint.

Passing mile marker five doesn't mean you finished the marathon. Don't slow down. Don't stop.

You Shipped. Are You Winning?

Remember, you are at the management evolution – so everything here is about looking backwards to inform decision moving forward. At this point, do you feel satisfied? You shipped. Are you winning?

Sometimes these are coupled and sometimes shipping and winning feel miles apart. Why? Because with being new at the LIFT Engineering System means the chaos isn't all shed off yet. LIFT is a system, and it takes time.

Win with Metrics That Matter

There are a host of metrics to choose from that will tell you if you are winning. After all, winning is all in the eye of the beholder – anyone can ship. Teams ship junk all the time, year after year. It doesn't matter because you aren't committed to that mediocrity. Most practitioners won't ever pick up a book on software at all. You, on the other hand, have read this book and are ready to keep going. Tables 8-1 and 8-2 list several metrics to choose from which become your internal Key Performance Indicators (KPI).

Table 8-1. Metrics that matter overall

Burn Downs	Cycle Time	Escaped Defects
Incidents	Availability	Support Emails

Table 8-2. Metrics that matter behavioral

Commits Per Day	Coding Days	Pull Requests Wait Time

From these brief, two tables, it's clear there are plenty of available metrics available to measure and move into your own internal scoreboard as KPIs.

Table 8-3 has even more, this time focused completely on the code base.

Table 8-3. Metrics that matter in the casebase

Test Coverage	Code Complexity	Tech Debt
Code Smells	Unit Test Failures	# Builds

Score Yourself

Here is how to use metrics to represent your KPIs and generate your scorecard:

1. Choose five metrics from the preceding lists as your KPIs.

2. Identify how to measure each KPI and ensure it won't take excessive effort to gather (delegate collection).

3. Set up a monthly schedule to gather the KPIs into a central location (just use a spreadsheet). This is your scorecard.

4. Review the scorecard monthly with other engineering leaders (developers, managers, ops, etc.).

That's it. Gathering and scoring KPIs isn't difficult once you've chosen some measurements and set up the process. This scorecard tells if you if you are winning beyond just shipping. This is how you will construct software and ship with high quality, consistently, inside the LIFT system.

▓ Make Sure You Can Measure It First

Choose the metrics that you can measure. For instance, don't choose code complexity unless you have a tool to measure it. Otherwise, the team will spin cycles messing around with plugins, open-source tools, and talking to tool vendors. Having good tools is important, but spin that work up separately, not as a development cycle.

Flatten the Ops Curve

Danger Will Robinson.

—The Robot, Lost in Space

We can measure system complexity through effort, number of components, or dollars spent. All three of these can meaningfully represent the concept of system complexity. We will measure this on the y-axis in Figure 8-3. The x-axis represents time.

The danger comes when the rate of operational complexity of a system scales linearly with the development complexity of the same system. This relationship doesn't need to be inverse, that would be impossible in modern systems, but it should not scale at the same pace. See Figure 8-3.

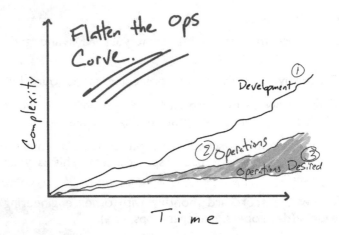

Figure 8-3. Flatten the ops curve

The black line (1) shows the complexity of the development effort over time. It will go up. You cannot stop this – any system where code and functionality are actively added or changed will have its overall complexity increase. Don't even try to bend this rule – it's like gravity.

Code is complex, and it grows. Why? Think about writing the algorithms for an investment application, which is the "domain" in Figure 8-4. These algorithms are created in code to reflect a mathematical methodology and set of calculations created by experts – the domain complex. Now, let's say we must model a one-year horizon and then a two-year horizon next month. Not a big deal, right? OK, now model a three-year investment horizon, including variables like income at retirement, retirement age, spousal income, number of dependents, and held-away assets. Yes, now we are playing with fire, and this code will be full of conditional statements, which is where software complexity originates. "If this, then that" is a powerful construct that holds the power of success or failure on every CPU clock cycle.

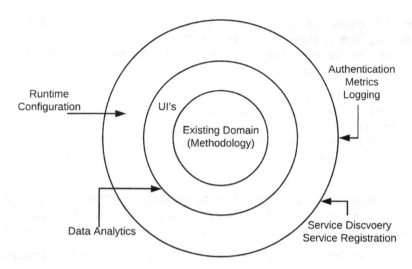

Figure 8-4. *The domain is where complexity belongs*

The red line (2) in Figure 8-3 highlights how operational complexity is increasing as development complexity increases. At first, this may sound logical. You may think:

More Code and APIs = More Operational Complexity

And, up to a certain point, that statement is true. But there should be a leveling out point where operations can scale without complexity. This is because adding 10K lines of code doesn't mean adding a new, different type of application server. Or, better yet, adding five new APIs as deployable services doesn't mean adding five new containers with different sets of configurations.

The operational footprint of a given system should strive for as much homogenous behavior and activity as possible.

For instance, sticking with APIs, when the deployment target is an Amazon Web Service Lambda Function behind and AWS API Gateway, the second API should be the same setup as the first. As well as the third, fourth, fifth, etc.

So, that is the first case.

The second case is when the operational team doesn't have control over their environment. Let's use an example with Kubernetes (pick your tech please for this analogy), and each deployment causes excessive scripting, configuration, and networking changes. This problem is more in the inability to operate the environment consistently versus however complex the code is. The deployable into an operational environment is some binary. The infrastructure doesn't know what's in the binary.

Figure 8-4 models a system in a basic onion architecture. Everything surrounding the nucleus of domain methodology is just technical noise. Customers are buying the domain first and the delivery of the functionality second. They aren't buying the operations at all – it's expense.

The threat of operational complexity is real. Many legacy systems suffer more from operational complexity than software complexity. Before you call this oxymoron, consider the rapid pace a developer could, if he or she chooses, refactor 1000 lines of code. Now, what about the rate of change to replace an old router, load balancer, three versions of tomcat, and CentOS in a production environment?

Yes, your assumption is correct. The operational complexity ends up being more expensive than the software complexity over time. On top of that, operational complexity reduces the rate of change to the software itself!

Summary: don't let operational complexity grow, flatten the curve immediately in the Manage evolution.

Shop at the Hat Store

After five evolutions, you have driven ambiguity out of planning, build, test, releasing, and operating software – but there is still more to eliminate. The next round of ambiguity is around roles that don't fit nicely into the development process.

Ambiguity in people's roles in a project can cause as much confusion as an undocumented API.

To solve this, be explicit with squads (small teams) working on projects and give everyone a role. Not a title. A title comes from HR and is usually tied to compensation. It's hard, like stone, and time-consuming to change. This really comes in handy when you have shared services, common code and operations spanning cloud and data centers.

Roles are soft. Roles are like hats – you put them on and take them off. LIFT doesn't have a prescription on the exact roles as they are closer aligned to individual team circumstances. Table 8-4 lists some examples.

Table 8-4. Roles

Role Name	Role Description
Engineering Service Lead (ESL)	An ESL leads and owns a shared service or common functionality. Consider, if three teams work on a web application that has stock pricing, who should own the pricing service? Assign an ESL.
Test Lead	The individual accountable for a given release to ensure all testing is completed and respected.
Performance Owner	This role assigns performance as a specialty so that one individual may oversee, inquire, and inform the overall performance of a system release.
Squad Lead	Small teams can't always self-organize. Use a Squad Lead to add structure to a squad.

Guided Autonomy

Forcing change doesn't work long term.

Guided autonomy means leadership supports independent decision-making within a set of guard rails. The guardrails exist to help teams not drive off the side of the road, crash, and burn (see Figure 8-5). Yes, the entire LIFT system provides some safety from chaos – and in this evolution, you reinforce team members' ability and need to make decisions.

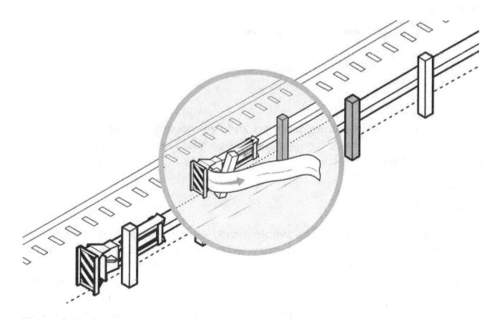

Figure 8-5. Guardrails prevent catastrophic endings

It's important to instill a sense of ownership into team members. To accomplish this objective in the manage evolution, remind them of the following:

- Team members are decisionmakers for decisions that belong to them. For example, no one is going to tell them to use bullets in acceptance criteria or write them as paragraphs.

- Projects don't need approval. They just need to follow onboarding and LIFT.

- The structure that the LIFT system offers is meant for teams to operate within side of.

Baby Names for Projects

Did you make it through an entire release cycle with project/release name "Sprint 85" or something like "HTML Output Upgrade"? If so, that stinks. Why? Because they are forgettable, boring, and uninspired. Oh, that's not enough reason? The names are also ambiguous.

Choose project names that the team won't mind saying (ever heard of fun, taskmaster?) and give the project some importance. So much of software development is rote and small in the scheme of things, so make the process more engaging by using words.

Examples:

- Project Three-Color Notebook
- Aardvark
- Oswald
- Project Zodiac

Some teams really like naming schemes and I've recently seen the schemes of: Norse Gods (think Thor's family) and videogames. The only way to go wrong here is to not pick names.

Tell a Story

Who doesn't like a story? The whole world exists through expression and story, so moving teams from system cycle to system cycle too requires some storytelling to keep them going. It's human nature to quit when you're winning until you start winning all the time. Think about someone trying to lose weight: they lose 3 lbs. and then stop the behaviors that got them there. It's self-sabotage. And software teams will look for excuses not to enter another system cycle because it takes work, and they are just barely winning by getting through the first couple of cycles. Maybe the win was just getting through the system cycle! Either way, express the pain which occurs sans LIFT System Engineering through story.

To help, I'll share a story. What follows is a true story with the names changed.

Several years ago, I led a development team focused on an extensive web application. The application was a public-facing website that made money off advertising and paid memberships. There was also a free version of the site with the usual paywalls, like any news/content site today. I took over this team moving from another team at the same firm. As soon as I walked into this group, multiple people told me: "please don't change the upgrade work the dev team is doing to the application from version 4.8 to 5.6. We must finish this upgrade."

This is not how I wanted to join this team, but we had a short history before, and there must be a good reason. So, I said, "OK, I'll be hands off since this is already a work in progress."

And that was one of the biggest mistakes of my career.

This team proceeded to deploy into staging environments and fail regressions. They had long development cycles. The exit criteria from QA were ambiguous. Roles were unclear. Product management already created a fixed data for this release – and they missed the date once before.

There wasn't one solid piece of evidence that this release would work ultimately, except that most functionality eventually passed QA. And I let it slide. I let it slide. I caved in to the pressure.

The team planned the release for a Thursday afternoon, starting around 4.30 PM, allowing traffic to trickle out allowing plenty of time for issue handling. They had DevOps, developers, product managers, and other stakeholders set up in a large war room environment, complete with six considerable screens in the front to toggle multiple laptops.

Six machines handled all the production load, and the team decided to take three machines out of rotation and deploy to those three, then swap them back in for the other three – all quite normal, until it wasn't.

With three machines back in production, the only three running the latest code with the upgrade to version 5.6, the worst thing happened on the big screen: we watched the nodes slowly maximize all CPU, then turn yellow, red, and then marked as dead. And the synthetic and manual testing proved out the same story.

OK, reboot those machines! They came back up, and as a trickle of traffic came into them, the same thing happened, yellow, red, and dead.

Well, there must be something wrong with these three. No problem, upgrade the other three and put those in production. Maybe it's a loaded thing – thinking that the small user load overwhelmed the new code. So, now all six machines are back in, all upgraded with the latest code, and slowly, yellow, red, and dead!

QA, what is going on?

"We don't know."

Developers, what is going on? "We don't know."

Ops, can you check the logs?

"We don't see anything."

At this point, I've told them to roll back. And the team does…and everything works. Therefore, it must have been bad circumstances or maybe a hardware glitch or a bad deployment. So, we repeat the deployment – three out, three in – and the same results…yellow, red, dead.

OMG.

The CEO walks in. Why?

Because the business head mentioned to him that this big release was going down, he came in to say congratulations to the utter dismay of the team, which included almost everyone who wrote code, tested, or project managed this significant upgrade effort. Did I mention they worked on this big release for five months?

We finally decide to roll back one more time, test, verify it's working as it was, and call it a night at 9 PM. And it's snowing. And life sucks.

I tell one of the senior engineers and the senior DevOps engineer to figure this out tomorrow.

The next day they figured it out. How? The developers added heavy logging statements around any server-side code that looked even remotely interesting.

Here was the deal: one each page load the user token for the user (free, paid, etc.) runs through an encryption library. Encryption is CPU expensive. Token encryption wasn't happening once a load, but instead, it was traversing a tree of components and running anywhere from 1-50 times per individual user page load. This meant, if ten users hit the site at once, around 500 encryption routines were running. Five hundred concurrent CPU-bound encryption operations were more than enough to max out the CPU and trigger the app server's runtime engine to shut down. And the bigger problem was this: the site handled 50 concurrent users with thousands of active sessions concurrently.

So, what is the lesson here?

First, do not ignore things that feel wrong. Listen to your gut more. Second, plan. Third, test. Fourth, log. Fifth, don't release when you know the software is not ready. If we had LIFT then, a prescriptive, pragmatic milestone-based approach using best practices at every level as opposed to ad-hoc faux agile processes that release would have been a success.

And these are the types of war stories to tell. The pain is the story. The pain drives team members to adopt practices that work. The pain is the selling point.

People

People power teams.

No people = No teams

We don't have a lot of assets as teams building software. What we have is our intellectual property (IP). IP comes from people. People make products and companies succeed or fail coupled with leadership support and vision.

I recently met someone who worked at an insurance company for 40 years. He's not retired yet, even though he was asked to take their separation package. Now he's consulting.

40 years.

He's a nice guy, but not someone you could spend a lot of time with. Why? He thinks his years of experience in one firm constitute varied experiences and attempts to speak into problems he knows nothing about. It's like a retired high school football coach telling you how to train for a triathlon because he used to have his team run sprints. He doesn't know anything about triathlons. You can't even listen to him because it comes from a place of ignorance.

Development

Then there is people development – the care, feeding, and growth of team members. Helping someone grow their career is important – we wouldn't be here without it ourselves. Watching someone with potential grow from a mid-level to senior engineer is satisfying and important work.

Don't bother developing no/low potential individuals. Think about it. If you have two people, professionals being paid a salary, and one has potential and the other is someone team members don't trust and has a bad attitude, well, which are you going to invest your time and the firm's funds into developing? Be honest. You know your answer. Save your money, the firm's funds are not for charity work.

S-Curves and People

S-curves are the common shape formed by projects when mathematically graphed.

The beginning, flat, left portion of the S denotes the introduction of a project and the team starting to form. Then the initial rise in output and cost (growth) is the middle part of the S with the max growth point named the *point of inflection*. And finally, the top part of the S is the plateau of output and productivity for the project. The curve of the S will eventually decline as entropy of a team weighs in and it's then required to start up a new project, to drive further growth.

Not having the right people in the right seats causes the initial flat portion of the S to elongate, as in Figure 8-6, which then means the project costs more money, or delivers fewer results, because it hits the first upward slope later than desired.

The following are a couple examples of right seat, wrong person:

Right seat: An engineering leader over the backend systems.

Wrong person: They are not bought into the vision, are monoculture, and inflexible.

Right seat: Principal Engineer

Wrong person: Inflexible, not willing to adapt and has their own agenda.

And here is an example of right seat, right person.

Right seat: Engineering Manager

Right person: They are aligned with the product vision, setting short and mid-term goals, and appreciate diverse views.

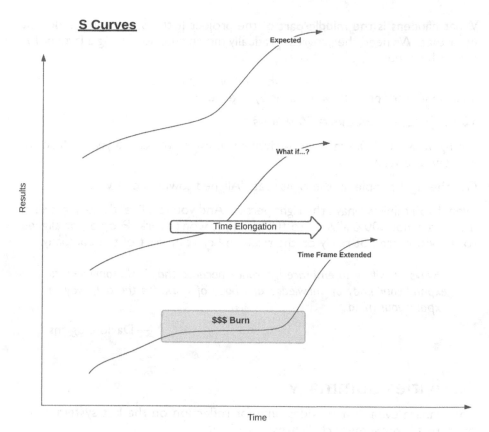

Figure 8-6. Using s-curves for projects

Figure 8-6 shows three s-curves. The first curve is a typical, normal project with the buildup, grow, and plateau scenario. The second curve from the top is the same as the first but suggests a time elongation scenario. And the third, bottommost s-curve displays the results when the project doesn't ramp up and grow because of the curve above it.

When the s-curve goes flat too long in the buildup, we lose both time and money. The loss of time is not recoverable. Time is finite. We miss markets, opportunities, and momentum to make a big rise in output.

The little decisions, the little battles, the "it's not a big deal if Karren is bought into the vision" all have consequences. These all contribute to flattening the s-curve and increase the risk of failure.

What happens if every project is extended by weeks/months simply because of miscommunication and because we have the wrong person in the seat? What if we have the wrong seat to begin with?

What happens is the middle part of the project flattens out and we do not want that. We need the progress gradually moving up, not taking a layover for a month or more.

Yet, this is exactly what happens when the wrong person is in the wrong seat. Imagine if every project, went over by five weeks.

10 projects x 5 weeks = 50 weeks

Losing 50 weeks in a year is non-trivial. How many weeks in a year? 52. So we lose about a year.

Get the right people. In the right seats. Aligned towards one vision.

Even if you think we have the right person. And you feel like it's the right seat. If they are not 100% aligned to the vision, it won't work. People not aligned to the vision are not really on the team and can't be part of the company.

> *Always be willing to embrace ignorance because that is the only way to expand your body of knowledge and body of work. It's the only way to expand your mind.*
>
> —David Goggins

Activities Summary

The manage evolution provides time for reflection on the last system cycle, executing improvement challenges:

- Fill out and use the Improvement Challenge document after system-cycle.

- Spend time to determine if what you are shipping is of value.

- Review and create the correct hat-based roles for your teams and projects.

- Give your projects a name. Things are real when they are named.

- Use the Manage evolution to tell stories and create new stories. Stories bring people together.

- Actively watch for elongated s-curves. Managed the slope of s-curves by putting the right people, in the right seats.

Summary

Stay the Course

The patterns of software construction in this book are simple, but not easy to implement. Therefore, the entire set of patterns are rolled into a progressive, step-by-step, system.

It will serve you well to remember that processes on their own are like trees. The system is made of those processes and is therefore the forest. Steering software projects from beginning to end requires us to look at the forest but still identify the types of trees living there.

Because software projects are rarely snowflakes, LIFT Engineering is both helpful and necessary.

LIFT can and will help you succeed consistently if you use the system and make it yours. Software projects are more similar than different and these problems are not going away. Projects follow the same cadence this system is built around, like Figure 9-1.

© Stephen Rylander 2022
S. Rylander, *Patterns of Software Construction*,
https://doi.org/10.1007/978-1-4842-7936-6_9

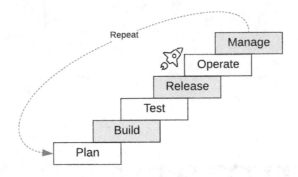

6 Evolutions = 1 System Cycle

Figure 9-1. LIFT Engineering Final View

At the end of the day, your teams and products get better through repetition. Repetition is a set of activities. Sets of activities are processes and sets of processes are a system. Tie all this together with planning, some discipline, iterative development, cohesive testing, visible roles, clear operational procedures, commitment to adapt and you will start winning more than you lose. Do this enough, and you'll win all the time.

I

Index

A

Acceptance Criteria (AC), 23, 50, 53, 55, 56, 58

Anti-corruption layer, 41–43, 51

Application Performance Management (APM) tool, 110, 111

B

Big Rocks, 21, 22, 24, 26

Build evolution
agile, 28
eliminate waste
beliefs, 48, 49
deploy, 51
patterns, 50
non-functional areas
debugging software, 39
defensive programming, 35–37
definition of done, 46, 47
logging statements, 37, 38
small functions, 40
performance, 44, 45
non-functional requirements pay, bills, 34
software, 33, 34
sprint success, 28–31

C

Continuous integration (CI), 46, 51

CPU clock cycle, 130

Craftsmanship, 2

D

Definition of Done (DoD), 46, 51, 90, 96

Domain Driven Design (DDD), 41, 43

E, F

Exception handling, 35, 36, 38

G, H

Gantt charts, 23

Globally unique identifiers (GUIDs), 42

Guard statements, 35, 36

I, J

Ignition document
change list, 84, 85
definition, 83
dependencies, 86
release details, 84
release script, 87
release summary, 83
risks/mitigation, 87
roles, 85, 86
rollback plan, 88
summary, 88

Improvement challenge, 126, 127

Intellectual property (IP), 137

© Stephen Rylander 2022
S. Rylander, *Patterns of Software Construction*,
https://doi.org/10.1007/978-1-4842-7936-6

Printed in the United States
by Baker & Taylor Publisher Services